GEORGE W MAC~ ...itions
handed dow ...l has
become one c ...n
Scotland. Geo. ...
memorable and ...ptivating any
audience, young ... ine world.

George has pu~ ...d two books of stories with
Luath Press, *Highland Myths and Legends* (2004) and
*Celtic Sea Stories* (2009, new ed. 2016) as well as
contributing to many magazines and papers. A
participant in the Scottish Storytelling Festival for many
years, he also organises the annual Skye and Lochalsh
Storytelling Festival and opened the Commonwealth
Heads of State Convention in Edinburgh with one of his
stories. George lives in Glendale on the Isle of Skye.

# The
# Old Grey Magician
## A Scottish Fionn Cycle

GEORGE W MACPHERSON

**Luath** Press Limited
EDINBURGH
www.luath.co.uk

First published 2016
Reprinted 2017
Reprinted 2018

ISBN: 978-1-910-745-41-0

The paper used in this book is recyclable. It is made from
low chlorine pulps produced in a low energy, low emissions
manner from renewable forests.

Printed and bound by
Bell & Bain Ltd., Glasgow

Typeset in 11 point Sabon and Libra by
3btype.com

# contents

# introduction

# a search
# for a story

We were sitting in the kitchen of my grandmother's old croft house on a cold dark winter's evening. The only light was provided by the peat fire and a rather smoky paraffin lamp. Silence lay on the room as my grand-uncles and my grand-aunt sat quietly after their meal, as was their custom.

I cracked the silent peace by asking a question.

'Why,' I said, 'did Black Duncan and Sorley say that the Mermaids of Ardnamurchan Point are the most beautiful but most evil in the world?'

After a second or two my grand-aunt Flora said, 'That's because they are but they aren't really Mermaids.'

My grand-uncle John cleared his throat and stroked his long white beard then spoke out. 'It came about this way and you are as well to know it from us for it is a family story.'

'A son of Fionn was captured by the Lochlannaich...' he began, then went on to describe how Fionn was unable to find a solution, then thought of asking for the aid of the Old Grey Magician and how the Magician appeared as soon as Fionn thought of him. He agreed to take on the task of saving the son of Fionn but to do so he had to fly as a bird to the court of Manannan, god of the sea, and get from him the use of his Mantle of Invisibility and Forgetfulness but to do this he had to do a task for Manannan.

Fionn also sent Comhnal Beul Airgod (Conval of the silver Mouth or Tongue) to negotiate with the Lochlannaich for time to carry out the rescue and he tricked the Lochlannaich so all that they got was the land between high and low water round the point of Ardnamurchan, so they lived on that land like Mermaids and Mermen.

Auntie Flora, who had put in bits and pieces, said, 'That is why, they aren't really Mermaids, they are descendants of the Lochlannaich with all their evil ways.'

This was in 1940 or 41 and I liked the story and tried to get more detail of how it all happened and where the Old Grey Magician went to and what powers he used, but my uncle seemed to be unwilling to go into detail and died not long after telling what he wanted of the story. My aunt was not for telling more, yet I felt there was more to be told.

I tried indirectly to get more about the Mermaids from one or two other storytellers in Ardnamurchan but got no more information. Then

in 1947 I was having a ceilidh in the house of a
cousin of my father, a man in his eighties and a
friend of his of a similar age was there. The two of
them were a great contrast. Niall was tall, well-
built and an ex-soldier who had served in the Boer
War and the First World War and had a rather
stern look to him. Lachie was small, light-built, full
of fun and always ready with a smile. He also
claimed to have been a 'genuine flyweight boxer'
and judging by his face he may well have been.

During the ceilidh, the talk turned to the
Mermaids of Ardnamurchan and Niall asked if
I knew how they were connected with Skye. I said
I had heard of them but didn't know much of any
Skye connection, though my aunt had said they
weren't real Mermaids.

This set off on a combined telling of how the
Old Grey Magician had gone from Skye to save
one of the Fianna who had been captured by
Lochlannaich. Niall included great detail of the
ceremonies carried out by the Old Grey Magician
and how he travelled to Eilan Mhannain to get the
Mantle of Manannan.

To get it, he had to carry out a task for
Manannan and save his son Honi, god of Seaweed.
Lachie came in with bits and pieces but took over

when it came to the Old Grey Magician calling on the Blue Men of the Minch and travelling below the sea. Both of them agreed that Conval of the silver tongue had tricked the Lochlannaich into getting only the land between high and low water round the point of Ardnamurchan and that the Mermaids of Ardnamurchan were the most beautiful and most evil in the world. Though both reckoned that it was a Skye story with very little connection to Ardnamurchan. However Niall did ask Lachie if he had in fact met up with the Mermaids while he was at sea, and was he was an old bachelor because of the fright they gave him. Lachie just laughed and said, 'It was more like yourself got the fright, Niall.'

After hearing the varied versions of the story I started to compare the similarities and the differences and how they fitted together to make a complete rounded story without cutting out or changing important facts and details. The stories did indeed combine pretty well seamlessly to become a complete story, so that the family stories from two areas again became one as they had been originally.

In 1954 I met up with a storyteller from the Isle of Man (a native Manx speaker) and he had a story of the Old Grey Magician getting a loan of the Mantle of Manannan. To get it he had to bring the Cup of Healing to Manannan. The Max speaker did not connect the story with Ardnamurchan but claimed the Old Grey Magician lived in Skye and flew to the Isle of Man as a great seabird. He also mentioned the great magic powers of the Old Grey Magician but did not know of the rituals for invoking them.

Putting it all together I felt I had arrived at a story which was very true to the original and did justice to it. As I had been given it as a family story in the beginning, I never told it outside the family until 2 November 2014 when I told it in the Netherbow Theatre along with Kati Waitzman.

I hope the written version will be enjoyed by all who read it.

After I first heard the story of the Mermaids of Ardnamurchan and their connection to the Old Grey Magician it kindled in me a desire to find more stories of him. This led to gathering stories pertinent to him and his ambivalent connection to Fionn. I soon discovered that these stories covered a very large area, especially areas known as centres of Druidical teaching such as Eilann Mhannan (Isle of Man), Eilean Sgiathanach (Isle of Sky or the winged isle) and Ardnamurchan, as well as

many other parts of Britain and Central Europe.
The Grey Magician's reputation as a Magician and
Healer was mentioned with awe in these stories,
yet there was always an element of fear too.
I collected stories of the Old Grey Magician, his
interaction with the Fianna and other beings on
land and sea and in doing so became aware of his
importance in the diaspora of the world.

In this book I tell some of his stories hoping
that they will arouse interest not only in the Old
Grey Magician, but also in the varied beings
involved with him, and that it will lead to his
stories being resurrected and collected in as near
to their original form as possible .

I am still hoping I might see some of the
beautiful Mermaids of the magical world of the
Magician, but not perhaps too close.

## the olò GRey magician

Who was or is the Old Grey Magician? This is a
subject on which both Academic and Oral
Research have so far failed to find a definitive
answer.

The Magician is found in different guises – both
male and female – in Welsh, Irish, Scottish and

Breton folk stories and legends. Many theories have been advanced to try to solve the riddle of his appearance and reappearance over many centuries. One such theory posits that it was merely a recurrent coincidence that a person with such powers appeared at various times and eras, but this stretches the bounds of coincidence to the breaking point considering the similarity of powers in each reoccurrence.

The theory which I feel has the greatest credence is one which takes into account the Druidical belief that there was no such thing as death, only change. The change was the death of the physical body, but when the body died Druids believed that the spirit did not die, instead transforming into a form of pure energy which soared away from the physical body to another plane of existence. A parallel existence from which it would return to this existence in a new body. In other words, reincarnation.

It was also believed that the greater the person was, the sooner they returned with their power enhanced. Greatness was not necessarily of a heroic nature, but encompassed healing, magic, prophecy etc and this reincarnation continued until the furthest plane of existence was reached, at which point the spirit would longer return to a new body.

In the case of the Old Grey Magician, many reincarnations with similar powers can be found through the centuries and it may well be that his final reincarnation was Michael Scott, The Wizard of the North. Much of this theory is my own, built up from the study of oral Druidic traditions. To expand the theory in order to attempt to come to a definitive conclusion would be the work of several years (some of which I have done) and would also require the publication of a book illustrating the possibilities of establishing such an interconnection between the physical and the spiritual worlds which, as more exploration of the universes continue, may well lead to a greater understanding of the Old Grey Magician's beliefs and perhaps endorse and confirm some of them.

# Sgiath's Sea Battle

hen Sgiath became Queen of Skye many neighbouring Kings felt that it was a slight to their prowess to have a Queen with an army of Amazon warriors ruling an area such as Skye.

Several of them challenged her right to rule and launched invasions on Skye but all were defeated and driven back to their own kingdoms.

There came a time, however, when several of the Kings and Lords of the lands in the north of Scotland came together and raised a great fleet of ships filled with an army of trained soldiers. Because they were coming from the sea to invade Skye, they were called Lochlannaich (which meant people from below the sea) and because of their strength and training they presented a great threat to Sgiath, causing her much anxiety and difficulty in forming plans to defeat such a force.

Eventually she decided her best chance lay in gathering a fleet herself and attacking on sea, hoping the element of surprise would work in her favour. Once her plan was formed, she put it into operation and soon had ships to carry her Amazons. She knew she was greatly outnumbered, but despite this when the invading ships were sighted she and her ships of Amazon warriors sailed out and gave battle to the fleet of Kings.

At this time the Old Grey Magician was sitting naked in the small cave behind Eas no Seallachd (the Waterfall of Sight). As he gazed into and through the waterfall he saw Sgiaths ships attacking the Great Fleet of the Kings and realised it was a brave but hopeless task.

*I must help my former apprentice*, he thought, *for she has become great and can be greater.* Without further thought he came from behind the waterfall, swimming through the pool of cleansing and even as he did so invoking the assistance of the god of Water and Air to assist him in the task he had put upon himself.

Turning into a seabird, the Old Grey Magician flew into the air heading southward to where the sea battle raged.

As he flew over the battle, he could see that while Sgiath's ships were fewer than those of the Kings they were faster and more manoeuvrable. But the greater numbers of the ships of the Kings were overpowering and sinking Sgiaths fleet despite the bravery of the Amazons.

He flew directly to the ship which Sgiath commanded and, landing on it, turned back to his

own shape and asked Sgiath if she wanted his help.
When she accepted his offer of help he told her to
tie a length of cloth to the bow of each of her ships.
Then he turned again to the seabird and flew to a
rock just off the coast which would be covered by
the sea at high tide. Standing naked on the rock, he
made his invocation to the Blue Men of the Minch:

> Blue Men of the Minch, my cousins of the sea,
> Listen as I call to you and answer to my plea
> I'll give to you a game to play I'm sure you will
>     enjoy
> For I will show you how, big ships you can
>     destroy

Suddenly Blue Men of the Minch appeared all
round the rock on which the Old Grey Magician
stood, and together they said:

> You call to put on us a task
> We'll do whatever you might ask
> You say it's something must be done
> And give us sport and lots of fun

The Old Grey Magician answered:

To sink some ships below the tide
A group must catch all on one side
Then pull the ship below the waves
And let them moulder in their graves
But ships with cloth upon their bow,
You must not touch them anyhow

The Blue Men of the Minch answered:

We hear the message that you give
That some will die and some will live
But with your words you set us free
To be the masters of the sea

The Blue Men of the Minch swam off and attacked
the ships of the fleet of the Kings with great gusto
and soon sank many of them. The remaining ships
of the Kings fled for safety and Sgiath was the
victor of the great sea battle. Only two prisoners
were taken by Sgiath's Amazons, and their fate is
another story.

# donnran
# [the brown
# searcher]

he Old Grey Magician was wandering across the hills as he often did, letting the spirits of nature guide him and listening to their voices. As he walked on he came across a young lad just past time of the rites of passage. The lad was sitting by a stream lost in some dream gazing upon a dragonfly.

The Old Grey Magician spoke to the lad and asked him what his name was and what he was doing. The lad said he was known as an 'aisling' (the dreamer) and he was doing just that: dreaming, as he always did, of how he could absorb the knowledge of all of nature both animal and plant. But though he tried, and listened to the voices of the insects and the bees and the plants and all the other sounds of nature, none made sense to him, though they gave to him a sense of peace.

'Come with me,' said the Old Grey Magician, 'and I will teach you how to hear what is being said to you and put you on the way to fulfilling your dream and becoming the greatest healer of all, though it will be a long hard road for you and once you set foot upon it you cannot turn back.'

'Gladly will I come,' said the lad. 'For you know my dream and I believe you when you say you can guide me to it. For that I will face any hardship.'

The Old Grey Magician led the lad back to his own place and taught him the languages of nature until the day came that the Old Grey Magician could teach him no more.

When that day came the Old Grey Magician took the lad to a waterfall and made the lad stand naked below the force of the water with his arms outstretched to the sides whilst he intoned an incantation which united the lad with the force of nature. When the lad could stand no more against the pounding of the waterfall the Old Grey Magician told him that now he must go and live naked in nature so that he could be given all the knowledge of nature including even the wisdom of the bees, and when the time came that the heat of the sun did not burn him nor the ice of winter chill him, then he would become known as the greatest healer of all.

So it came about that the lad, Donnran, now a grown man, became known first of all as a strange hermit who lived naked on the moors and was regarded by many as mad, until the day came when he was hailed as the greatest healer of all. This came about because of his Healing of Caoilte the swiftest runner of all the Fianna.

It came to pass that during one of the battles of

the Fianna Caoilte the swiftest runner of all the
Fianns was badly wounded in the leg. He was
carried to the place of Fionn and the best
physicians came to cure his wound, but none
could, for it appeared that the weapon which had
wounded him had been poisoned and no matter
what they did it got worse to the point that the
physicians felt the only way to save him was to cut
off his leg. But Caoilte said he would sooner die
than lose his leg.

The Old Grey Magician told Fionn that if he
wanted to save Caoilte he must send two of the
Fianna to find Donnran and ask him if he would
come to the place of Fionn and heal Caoilte, for
only he could do it.

Fionn sent two of his most trusted followers to
search for Donnran and ask him to come and heal
Caoilte for no one else could. After much searching
the Fianns found Donnran and put to him the
request of Fionn. Donnran agreed to go with them
and do all he could to heal Caoilte.

When they reached the place of Fionn, Donnran
went straight to the chamber where Caoilte lay and
looked upon the great wound in the leg of Caoilte.
The flesh in the wound was black and green with
rivulets of yellow pus running through it, and the

smell coming from the wound could make strong men sick.

Donnran looked into the face of Caoilte and said to him, 'Do you believe I can heal you?' Caoilte looked into the eyes of Donnran and said, 'Yes I believe you can.'

Donnran told Fionn, 'You must send two of your men up over the ridge of Beinn an Uisge. There they will find a small Lochan and beside it will be lying the body of a stag which has been dead for some time. It will be crawling with maggots, and what they must do is cut off its right rear leg, wrap it in a skin which I will give them, and bring it to me here.'

Fionn immediately sent two of the Fianna to carry out the instructions of Donnran, and it was not long till they found the stag which Donnran had told them about. Despite the smell of rotten flesh, they cut off the right rear leg of the stag and wrapped it in the skin then carried it down to where Caoilte lay.

Donnran took the skin with the leg inside into the chamber of Caoilte and laid the skin flat, then held the leg of the stag above it and gave it a strong thump with his fist. Dozens of maggots fell from the leg and onto the skin. Donnran carefully scooped a double handful of them then walked across to where Caoilte lay and he put the maggots into the great wound in Caoilte's thigh. Then he laid wet docken leaves over the wound and tied them down with rags.

Next morning Donnran removed the rags and the docken leaves and carefully scraped the maggots from the wound. Already there was a difference; the blackness and yellow pus were almost gone. Donnran wrapped the maggots, leaves and rags he had removed from the wound, and told the Fianns to burn them. Then again he smote the leg of the stag over the skin and scooped a double handful of the maggots and laid them into the wound in Caoilte's thigh, covered them with wet docken leaves and tied them down with rags.

This time he left the dressing in place for two days and when he removed it and removed all maggots from the wound, the wound was clean fresh flesh and the smell was gone. Donnran then gently and carefully spread over the clean flesh an ointment he had brought with him made of the jelly of the bees and again over the wound he tied wet docken leaves bound with rags. The dressing and maggots he had removed from the wound were again burned.

After another two days he removed the dressing from the wound and now it could be seen that the flesh in the wound was growing and filling the wound. Donnran cleaned the wound carefully then smeared over the new flesh another ointment he had brought made from the honey and wax of the bees, covering it again with wet docken leaves tied down with rags. Once again the dressing from the wound was burned.

This time the dressing was left undisturbed for three days. When Donnran again removed the dressing and cleaned the wound it was nearly closed, and Donnran spread over it yet another ointment made from honey of the bees, pollen of certain flowers and water from a well of healing.

'Now,' said Donnran, 'you must remove this dressing after another three days and you will find hardly even a scar left of the wound. Wash it with the water of the healing well which I will leave with you. The day after you have done this Caoilte can stand on his feet again and soon he will run as he ran before and the wind before him he will catch, but the wind behind him will not catch him. I will go back now to live close to nature for my work here is done.'

So it was and Caoilte became again the greatest

runner of all the Fianna, and Donnran was hailed as the greatest healer of all, yet continued to live close to and learn from nature.

# the feeling
# of fear

*I heard this story in Ardnamurchan from a
man who came originally from Caithness
who said he had it from his Grandmother
who was from Thurso.*

*He also claimed that the baby the Old
Grey Magician took from the cave became
the Grainne involved in the death of Diarmid.*

Somewhere in Sutherland lived a clan of
robbers who were a thorn in the side of
every settled clan in Scotland. Even
Fionn and his Fianna had been unable
to track down the robbers and bring
justice upon them.

The robbers, over the years, had become more
and more brutal and audacious as their hiding
place remained undetected. Now they had
slaughtered a whole family of men, women and
children and Fionn had decided that enough was
enough, and that the clan of robbers must be
found and punished. As he and his followers had
been unable to do this he called on the Old Grey
Magician, asking him to be successful where he
and his men had failed.

The Old Grey Magician said he would take the

task upon himself but Fionn and the Fianna must accept any punishment he put upon the robber clan if he could not get them to surrender to the justice of the Fianna. Fionn agreed to this but reminded the Old Grey Magician that under the law of the Fianna they must be given a chance to speak on their own behalf.

The Old Grey Magician went back to his own place and there he made rituals and incantations to help him in his quest, and made offerings to and asked the assistance of the gods. Then he travelled to the wilds of Sutherland posing as a storytelling bard and musician. He was indeed a good roving troubadour and soon became known to the people of the area. Then one evening a stranger came to him and asked him to go with him and play for his people. When the Old Grey Magician said he was a bit tired and would rather wait till the next day the stranger gave a whistle and more men appeared around them, all well-armed, and told him he either came with them now or his blood would stain the heather.

'Would you break the law and kill a storyteller?' said the Old Grey Magician. 'What kind of men are you?'

'We are men who live by our own laws and pay

no heed to any others,' they said, so the Old Grey Magician pretended to fear them and went with them. As the darkness had come down the storyteller had difficulty in discerning where they were going, yet realised that it boded ill for him that they were not hiding the route from him by more effective means than the dark of the night, but he went on with them for now he was sure they were of the ones he wanted.

Before too long they came to a narrow gully which led into a dark cave. Once they were in the cave, torches of pinewood were lit to guide them on their way. They went through a winding tunnel till they came to a huge cavern lit by many torches. In the cavern were many people: men, women and children. The Old Grey Magician was led into the centre of the space and ordered to entertain them; he told a story of the Fianna then sang a ballad of the deeds of the gods to which he added soft music of the highland flute, and they were well pleased. But then he spoke of what they were and told them that they should surrender themselves to the mercy of the Fianna for they would be given a fair trial by the Fianna with the right to speak on their own behalf and put forward their own side of the story. The people laughed at him, they said 'We have our own laws, and to show Fionn how little we think of his we will send back your head as a present,' and they started to reach out to grasp him.

The Old Grey Magician spun round in a circle with his Wand of Peeled Rowan pointing to the floor and where it pointed flames rose from the floor so that he was protected by a ring of fire.

'I am the Grey Magician,' he said. 'I have come here to give you the chance to leave and surrender to Fionn. If you do not take it I will deal to you the punishment you deserve. Any of you who wish to leave now can do so and I will grant them safe journey to Fionn.'

The robber clan laughed at him again, saying, 'We have killed many such as you. You are one old man and your magic will not save you.'

'I gave you your chance,' said the Old Grey Magician, and he pointed his wand toward the entrance to the cave. Two lines of fire sprang up and he walked between them to the passageway entrance then turned and faced the people. 'Your judgement is on your own heads,' he said, raising his foot and stamping on the ground. As he did so, a tremble ran through the cave and one or two rocks fell from the roof. People screamed, but the Old Grey Magician did not listen to the screams

but stamped twice again with his foot making the
roof and walls of the cave collapse, burying all
within so that silence reigned. As the Old Grey
Magician turned to leave he heard the cry of a
baby and saw in a niche in the passageway wall a
baby who was only a day or two old, he picked it
up saying, 'Surely you are meant for great things
when you alone are left alive. I must be meant to
see you are raised.'

The Old Grey Magician returned to the court of
Fionn to tell Fionn his problem was solved, and
from that time on there was always a feeling of
fear when dealing with the Old Grey Magician.

# the daughter
# of the king
# of spain

*This story came from two sources, one in Ardnamurchan and one originally from Mull. The only differences in their stories were that the man from Mull insisted it was Iain Ruagh MacLean who handfasted the princess and took her to Duart Castle whilst the Man from Ardnamurchan claimed it was the King of Morvern and Mingarry Castle.*

*Handfasting, an important term in this story, was a form of engagement or trial marriage, usually lasting a year. Today some people use the handfasting ceremony, which involves the couple's hands being bound together with cord or rope, as part of their wedding ceremony.*

ow the King of Morvern, or some say Iain Ruagh of Duart chief of the Macleans, went to Spain and handfasted with a daughter of the King of Spain.

The daughter of the King of Spain travelled back to Mingarry Castle or Duart Castle and hopes were great that she would have a son and the handfasting would become a marriage.

Things went well with the couple and they became deeply in love, yet time moved on and time changes everything. After six months of the handfasting the daughter of the King of Spain was not pregnant and she was ill. Very ill and likely to die.

Her lover was distraught and called all the known physicians to cure her but none could, and all agreed she would soon die.

MacLean of Duart or the King of Morvern, now in a last desperate attempt to save her, asked the Old Grey Magician to help in the hope that he could succeed where others failed.

The Old Grey Magician came and looked on the King of Spain's daughter then turned to her lover and said, 'I can cure her but to do this you must make what I ask and allow the Princess to go with me to Spain where the Great Doctor of Spain I and can cure her. Then I will bring her back to you.'

'To have my Princess cured,' said her lover, 'I will do all that you request.'

The Old Grey Magician then asked that a stone coffin be carved from a single piece of rock, and that it must be big enough to hold the Princess lying down and another person sitting at one end.

Although surprised, the lover of the Princess of
Spain ordered the workers in stone to make such a
coffin and to do it as quickly as possible, in fact to
work without ceasing till the job was done.

The masons worked without stopping and in
three days the coffin was carved. Then on the
orders of the Old Grey Magician it was carried to
the shore and placed at a point below the high tide.

Once the coffin was in position the Old Grey
Magician went to the chamber of the King of
Spain's daughter and asked her if she believed he
could cure her. When she said she did he massaged
all her body with a special oil then wrapped her in
An plaide bhan Dhruidean (the fair plaid of the
Druids), and carried her down to the stone coffin
and laid her in the bottom of it. As he did so a cat
leapt into the coffin and snuggled down beside the
Princess.

'Let it be,' said the Old Grey Magician, 'it has a
task.'

Then, as the tide rose, the Old Grey Magician,
sitting at the end of the coffin, intoned an
incantation in such a way it could not be heard by
those on the shore and to their amazement the
coffin – which should have sunk – floated on the
crest of the waves and directed by a flourish of the

Magician's hand was soon lost to the view of those on the land.

The stone coffin carrying the Old Grey Magician, the Princess and the cat cruised steadily over the surface of the sea until it arrived on a beach in Spain. There the people who saw this strange sight reported it to the King of Spain and he, with his bodyguard, came to investigate this mystery. To the King's great surprise he found his daughter in the coffin. The Old Grey Magician told the King that his daughter was dying but that if the King would allow the Great Doctor of Spain to help him, between them they could cure her.

The King of Spain said he would only allow the Great Doctor of Spain to help the Old Grey Magician if he would solve a problem for him and for Spain.

'Tell me your problem,' said the Old Grey Magician, 'it may be that I can solve it.'

The King told him that a plague of rats had come into Spain and were eating all the food that was stored for the winter, even the food in the storehouses of the King, and they could not be stopped. The Old Grey Magician smiled and said 'The solution for that came with me,' and he reached into the coffin and brought out the cat.

'Here is your solution,' he said, 'for this cat by itself will kill many of your rats and it will soon have kittens who before long will also kill rats as will all the descendants of the cats.' He put the cat on the ground and within seconds it was killing rats to the delight of the King.

The King allowed the Great Doctor of Spain to work together with the Old Grey Magician and between them they healed his daughter. Once she was cured and the cat and her kittens were killing the rats as the Old Grey Magician had said they would, he and the daughter of the King of Spain got back into the coffin and the coffin floated again on the crest of the waves carrying them safely home to Scotland.

The Princess went back to her lover and had a fine baby boy, yet they never married though they had other children. It was whispered that the princess (whose mother was the daughter of two Macphersons who had lived in France then moved to Spain and married the King of Spain, so their daughter had been made a Dame of Spain but had kept her grandparents' name) didn't marry because her first boy was of the seed of The Old Grey Magician.

When the Daughter of the King of Spain died

she was buried in the stone coffin which would one day take her back to Spain.

The totem animal of the clan Macpherson is the wildcat.

# the tribe of fife

*Gavran is also sometimes spelled Gabhroinn or Gabhran. In some versions the king is called Gartnach, which would make the story much older.*

When Gavran was King of Scotland he had to fight many risings by various tribes who did not want him as king. Most of these rebellions had been crushed by the superior might of his army, but now Gavran and his kingdom, which he ruled from his fortress in Dunadd, were facing his most serious challenge. A tribe called Tuatha Fiodgha (the Tribe of Fife) had risen up against him. Of all the area's tribes they were the most feared for they coated their weapons with a poison so powerful that the slightest scratch caused paralysis, leading to death.

King Gavran knew that he was facing defeat, and thus the end of his kingdom, at the hands of Tuatha Fiodgha, for they had never been defeated in a battle before and were regarded as invincible. He had to devise a plan to beat them, but he had no idea how this could be done. All he had to hearten him was the loyalty of his army's leaders, who said they would fight to death, as he would himself.

He made up his mind that he and his men would face Tuatha Fiodgha on the Moss of Dunadd despite the likelihood of a defeat that would end their way of life.

As Gavran sat in the hall of Dunadd, in the deepest gloom he had ever felt, in front of him there suddenly appeared a' Bhuidhseir Glas (the Old Grey Magician) and he said to the king, 'All you need to do to get my help is ask.' The king was surprised but immediately said 'I need all the help I can get and yours would be more than welcome, for I have heard of your great powers.'

The Grey Magician then told the king that he must carry out the work the Grey Magician instructed him to do, and if he did so he might well achieve victory over the Tribe of Fife.

The king agreed and called out to his men, telling them to carry out the work that the Grey Magician commanded.

The Grey Magician told the men to start digging a large circular pit, about four feet deep and twenty-five feet across. Once they had dug it the bottom had to be coated with clay, and the sides lined with timber and clay so that it was watertight.

When the pit was finished they had to gather mares' milk from all over the kingdom to fill the pit. The men did as ordered by the Grey Magician, and as they filled the pit with mares milk the Grey Magician stood at the side of the pit, uttering an incantation and casting handfuls of herbs into the milk.

He then told the king that when the Tuatha Fiodgha attacked, any men of the king's army wounded by the weapons of the Men of Fife were to be thrown in the pit. This would heal them and they could fight on.

The following day the Tuatha Fiodgha attacked and several of the king's men were hit by their poisoned weapons. They were thrown into the pit, and they emerged ready to fight again. The Tuatha Fiodgha were astounded to see men they thought should be dead coming back full of life and ready to fight them. As the battle went on, the Men of Fife realised that their poison no longer worked and panic set in. They turned and ran, but many of them were caught and slaughtered by the king's army. It was the end of any attempt by the Kingdom of Fife to usurp the Kingdom of

Scotland. Gavran's reign from that time on was long and peaceful.

The Grey Magician disappeared when he saw the outcome of the battle, but from that time on he was held in great esteem in all of Scotland. However, he was also greatly feared.

# the cup of healing:
## cupan beatha

*From this story in later years was developed
the story of the knights of King Arthur.
Diamaid became Sir Galahad, the most
gallant of knights. The Cup of Healing
became the Holy Grail and the search for it
and the adventures involved was also
incorporated into the Arthurian myth.*

*I was told this story originally by two old
men in Ardnamurchan. They were two
brothers who lived together and at the time
of telling the story to me they were in their
late eighties and I was about twelve years old.*

t had been a long hard day of hunting in the
Cuillins. One of those days in Skye when the
mist was heavy and wet and it soaked you
right through to your skin. Fionn and the
other Fianna had been hunting all day and
now were heading back tired, wet and dreary too.
When they reached the place they were camping
the covers had been put up, the fires were lit and
they had food to eat and wine and other things to
drink. They made merry and then as the night
came down heavier they retired under the covers.

And as Fionn was lying there he heard a

scratching noise near his cover. He lifted the edge of the cover and looked, and there was the ugliest woman he had ever seen in his life. She was old, wrinkled and twisted. Her face was covered with warts and pustules. Her nose ended in a great hook and her chin came up to meet it. She said to Fionn, 'Please let me under the cover. I want to get out of this terrible wind and rain. Just let me into a corner.'

Fionn looked at her and said, 'You ugly old hag, I would not let you under the covers even if you were my mother. Get away from me.' And the old woman sadly went away. She came to the cover of Ossian. He was sleeping soundly wrapped in his plaid beneath the cover. When he heard the scratching on his cover he looked and there was this ugly old hag of a woman. The ugliest woman he had ever seen in all his born days. She said to him, 'Please let me come under the covers, just into a corner out of this terrible weather.' Ossian looked at her and said, 'No, you are the ugliest most horrible looking woman I have ever seen in my life. I will not let you under the covers even into a corner. Get away from me.' The old hag looked even sadder and moved away. Ossian put down the edge of the cover again.

Caoilte was lying sleeping soundly dreaming of the hunt in the hills when he heard this scratching on his cover. The scratching went on and on until he could no longer disregard it. He went across and lifted the corner of the cover and there was the hag. The most dreadful looking woman he had ever seen in his life. Wrinkled and twisted, horrible to look upon. Her face covered with warts and pustules. Caoilte looked at her and said, 'What do you want?'

The woman said, 'Please let me in just under a corner of the cover, so that I can be dry for this one night. Please let me in?'

Caoilte looked at her and said, 'No. No I will not let you anywhere near me. You are the most horrible looking hag I have ever seen in my life. I would not have you even in the least corner of my cover. Get away from me and don't come back again.' He put down the corner of the cover and the old hag sadly went on her way.

She came to the cover of Diarmaid and she scratched on the cover and Diarmaid woke and looked out and he saw the old hag there. She said to him, 'Please let me come under a corner of your cover. Just let me be get warm there, let me be dry out of this terrible weather.' And Diarmaid was not only the bravest and the most handsome of all the Fiann, he was also the most tender hearted. He looked at her and said to her, 'You are the most horrible looking hag I have ever seen in my life but you shall have a corner of the cover. I would turn no one away on a night such as this.' And he allowed the old woman to come in and go into a corner of the cover. The old woman settled into a corner and Diarmaid wrapped himself back into his plaid and lay there comfortably. After a little while he heard the old woman saying, 'Oh Diarmaid, Diarmaid, please let me under your plaid, just a little bit to give me some warmth. I am so cold here because I was soaked outside. I am so cold. Just give me a corner of your plaid to keep me warm.'

Diarmaid looked at her and once again he said, 'You are the most horrible looking hag I have ever seen in my life but I can see you are cold and shivering and wet. I will let you come under the plaid with me but try not to come against me. I would not like the feel of you against me at all.' The old woman lifted part of the plaid and slipped under beside Diarmaid. And as soon she slipped under the plaid she turned into the most beautiful woman that Diarmaid had ever seen in all his life.

And so the two of them had a wonderful night together both wrapped into the plaid of Diarmaid. In the morning Diarmaid got up, folded his plaid into his phillimore and put it on and went out, and with him walked the beautiful woman he had slept with the night before. The first person he met was Fionn. Fionn looked and said to the woman, 'You are the most beautiful looking woman I have ever seen in my life. Oh, if you were to come to me I would shelter and help you.'

The woman looked at him and said to him, 'Fionn, you had your chance last night and you cast me out.' As they continued on they met Ossian. Ossian looked at the woman and he said to her, 'Ah, you are the most beautiful looking woman I have ever seen in all my life. If you were to stay with me, all the poetry I would write for you, the most beautiful poems you ever heard in your life, wonderful poems of the hunt and love I would write for you.'

'Ha!' said the woman. 'Ossian, you had your chance last night and you threw me out.' And they continued on and met Caoilte. Caoilte looked at the woman and he said, 'You are the most beautiful, the most wonderfully formed woman I have ever seen in all my born days. If you were mine I would hunt the hill for you, I would outrun the deer and bring them to you so you would never want.'

'Ha!' said the woman. 'You had your chance last night Caoilte and you threw me out.' And they carried on.

Diamaid and the woman passed out of the camp followed by a great bitch, Diarmaid's hunting dog. This great bitch was heavy with pups. The woman said to Diarmaid, 'Diarmaid, what would you like most in this world?'

Diarmaid said, 'Well, I would love to have a fine castle down near the shore and in the castle I could live happily with you for as long as we would both be together we could be happy. But also with my dog and its pups.'

The woman said, 'Is that the wish of your heart Diarmaid?'

'It is indeed.' said Diarmaid.

'Well,' said the woman, 'I could give you your wish but you must remember that you must never cast up to me of how I was when you first saw me.'

Diarmaid promised he would never cast this up to her and would always be faithful and true to her.

They camped out for the night on the hill and in the morning when they woke up down there above the shore was a huge fine castle. They walked into the castle and Diarmaid's faithful hound followed him in. In the castle was everything he could wish for, all the very best of furnishings. Diarmaid and the woman settled down there and lived very happily together.

Diarmaid said to the woman, 'There is one thing you must never do. You must never give away any of my dogs.'

Diarmaid went out hunting again and the bitch had two pups. Diarmaid left the two pups in the care of the woman. And as he went out he said, 'Remember, you must never give away any of my dogs.'

The woman stayed in the castle with the dogs when a man came to the door and asked for hospitality. And as was the custom hospitality was given. He came in, was fed and given a bed for the night. In the morning the woman said to him, 'What gift will you have from the house?' For it was a custom that a guest leaving the house would always be given a gift. And a gift would be what he or she asked for.

The man looked at her and he said, 'There is just one gift I would like. Give me one of the pups.'

The woman said, 'I can't give you that. These

are the pups from my husband's bitch and he would not be very pleased at all if I gave you one.'

The man said, 'Would you break the custom of years? I am sure your husband would be very insulted if you broke the great tradition.' The woman thought to herself, *Well, if I give him one pup we still have the other pup and the bitch. Surely Diarmaid can stand with that.* And she gave the man one of the pups.

When Diarmaid came back from the hill and discovered that one of the pups was gone he said to the woman, 'What have you done with my pup?'

The woman said to him, 'A stranger came here and requested hospitality and in the morning he asked for a pup as his gift.'

Diarmaid said, 'You silly fool. You clown of a woman. What do you think of giving him one of my pups? I told you, you are never to give away any of my dogs. And to think, that you who were nothing but an ugly old hag when I first saw you should do a thing like that to me.'

The woman said, 'That is the first time.'

Life went on with them. They were living happily there and Diarmaid again went to the hill with the bitch. The woman was in the castle by herself and there came a stranger to the door and asked for hospitality. He was granted hospitality and in the morning on leaving he was asked what gift he would have.

He said, 'The gift I would have is that pup. She is a nice little pup.'

The woman said, 'No that gift I cannot give. The pup is my husband's.'

The stranger said, 'You would break the laws of hospitality? You would insult this house? Insult your husband by refusing me the gift I asked for?'

Once again the woman thought, *Diarmaid himself would not break the law of hospitality of the house. He would not give up the great tradition.* And again she gave the pup to the man.

When Diarmaid came back from the hill he was even more angered than before. 'What have you done with my pup?' he asked.

The woman told him that a stranger had come and demanded the pup as a gift.

Diarmaid said to her, 'I told you, you are never to give away any of my dogs. You, you would do this to me and I was so kind to you when you were nothing but a dirty, wet sniffling old hag. I took you in.'

The woman said, 'That is the second time.'

A few days later Diarmaid was away with some

of the other Fianna. He left the bitch at home in the castle with the woman when an old woman came to the door and asked for hospitality. The woman took the old woman in and gave her hospitality of the best she had. The next morning as the old woman was leaving the woman asked, 'What gift will you have?'

The old woman looked at her and said, 'The gift I would have is that bitch, the brindle bitch of Diarmaid.'

Diarmaid's woman looked at the old woman, 'No, I can not give you that gift as it is my husband's most prized dog. She is everything to him.'

The old woman looked at her and said, 'You would stop me having the bitch and yet your husband himself would not stop me having it. He maintains all the great traditions. He is the most hospitable man who ever walked this earth and you would have me believe he would not grant the gift of hospitality?'

Once again the woman thought, 'Well, this is true enough of Diarmaid.' And she gave the old woman the bitch.

When Diarmaid came back he went into the castle and he immediately said, 'Where is my bitch? What have you done with her?'

The woman told him how the old woman had come and asked for the bitch as a gift. Diarmaid was furious. He said to her, 'You clown, you fool. What have you done? You have given away my bitch. The best dog ever I had. You, you would do this to me? You, whom I took in when no one else would take you in, when you were such an ugly hag of a woman that no one wanted to let you touch them. And only I let you join me in my plaid.'

The woman said, 'That is the third and the last time.'

Diarmaid and the woman went back to bed that night but in the morning when Diarmaid woke up the woman had gone and so had his castle. All that was left of it was a mark in the ground where it had been. Diarmaid was broken hearted, for he dearly loved the woman. He decided he would follow her tracks to wherever they would lead him. He started to follow her tracks. He went on and the tracks led far away. They went across and then down towards the sea at a different stretch of coast. As he went he found gout of blood at the side of the track. He picked it up and put it in his dorlainn, the leather satchel which was carried at the belt. And he carried on. Then he found a second gout of blood, he picked it up and put it into the dorlainn. Then he reached the sea, and there at the side of the sea was a third gout of blood. Diarmaid picked it up and put it into his dorlainn and carried on into the sea. As he moved into the sea, the sea opened in front of him as if it was a tunnel going down below the water.

Diarmaid walked down the tunnel. He carried on walking down the tunnel until he came to a place, a great city below the sea all built of shining white marble with people in the streets, everyone looking happy. Diarmaid carried on until he came to the greatest building in the place. When he arrived at the greatest building the doors were flung open and he went inside.

Inside, the king of the Under-Sea-Land said to him, 'What have you done to my daughter?' Then the king led Diarmaid to a bedchamber and there lay the beautiful woman dying. Diarmaid was broken hearted now and said to the king, 'How can I save her? If there is anything I can do to save her I will do it.'

The king said, 'There is only one way you can save her, you must go and get the Cup of Healing. It is the cup that heals all ill. You must go and get it and bring it back here. I will then fill it with water and you must crush into the cup the three gouts of blood and let the woman drink it. But when she does this, all her love for you will turn into hate and you will never see her again.'

Diarmaid said, 'I am the one who has wronged her and I love her so much that I will do even this although I will lose her.'

The king then told Diarmaid that to get the Cup of Healing he must go to another island on which he would meet dangers and adventures. On that island, right in the centre, he would find the cup of healing on an altar of the druids, but the cup was protected by a great serpent. Diamaid would have to overcome the great serpent to get the cup of healing.

Diarmaid bade farewell and went on his way. Once again he walked under the sea in what seemed like a tunnel of water until he came to the island of Hrumm. And on the island of Hrumm, as he walked across the land he saw a river and sitting beside the river was a little man all dressed in brown. Diarmaid looked at the river and saw it was fast flowing and rough. He knew that he would get thoroughly wet and perhaps carried away trying to cross it. The little man looked at Diarmaid and said, 'I see, you are not very keen on crossing the water.'

'Well', said Diamaid, 'I want to cross it right enough but I don't want to get myself and my equipment soaking if I can avoid it.'

'Well you can avoid it.' said the little man. 'I'll carry you across.'

Diarmaid looked at the little man and said, 'You are a quarter of the size of me, you could never carry me especially across a river as fierce as that!'

'Oh I could.' said the little man. 'But if I do it you must make me a promise.'

'What is the promise?' asked Diarmaid.

'When you come back with the cup', said the little man. 'You must allow me to drink from it.'

'Well', said Diarmaid. 'I am sure that can be arranged. I can promise that.'

And with that the little man picked Diarmaid up on his shoulders. Then he ran across the surface of the water and put Diarmaid down at the far shore.

The little man said, 'There you are now, carry on your way but remember your promise.'

Diarmaid carried on his way. He walked on for some miles until he came to the great square altar of the druids. As he had been told, on top of the altar curled all round was a serpent. Diamaid had never known or seen a serpent this huge in all his life. The serpent was wide awake and his tongue flicked in and out and his eyes watched Diarmaid. Behind the snake, standing in the centre of the altar, was the Cup of Healing, but all around the cup were the coils of the serpent. Diarmaid looked and thought; *Now if I take my sword and try to cut the head of the serpent I am not sure I could cut it off with one blow because of the sheer size of it. How am I going to get to that cup?*

Then he remembered the woman lying there and the state she was in and at that his heart swelled and his courage came back to him and he made the great leap of the heroes and landed in the coils of the serpent. He picked up the cup and carried, with the same leap, the cup out of the coils over the serpent's head and landed safely.

He tucked the cup into his dorlainn and started to walk back across the island. But this time he walked a different route so that he would not meet up with the little brown man. For he knew that this little man was one of the fairy people and if he gave the little man a drink from the cup he would lose the cup and never see it again. He took a different route around, up over the hills and down again to the sea where he had first come out. Once

71

again, when he walked into the sea it was as though a tunnel came around him, a tunnel made of water, and he walked through the tunnel down deep into the sea until he came again to the great white city. When he arrived at the Great White City he walked into the shiny palace of the king and said to him, 'I have the cup.'

The king said, 'I will fill it with water and you must crush the gouts of blood into the water.'

The king filled the cup with water and Diarmaid crushed the gouts of blood into the cup and stirred them in well with the water. Then he went to the chamber where the woman was lying. Diarmaid looked at her. She was so beautiful lying there despite her illness that he thought, *If I give her a drink from the cup she will hate me and I will never see her again. Can I stand that? Would it not be better not to let her drink and I might perhaps have some little time of happiness left with her?*

But then he thought to himself, *No. This is my fault. I am to blame for all this. If I had not acted as I did she would still be with me.*

He bent forward and propped her up in the bed and gave her a drink from the cup. The moment she drank from the cup, she became well again and she looked at Diarmaid and said to Diarmaid, 'You,

you are nothing to me now. Go from me, I never want to see you again.'

Diarmaid turned and walked out of the chamber, saddened and distressed. When he walked out of the chamber the king was there and he said to him, 'I told you Diarmaid that if you gave her a drink from the cup she would hate you and you would never see her again. But you have done your very best for my daughter. You have done what a good man should and so I will give you something, Diarmaid that will make up for losing her. It is a gift for you.'

The king put his finger into the centre of the forehead of Diarmaid. When he took the finger away there it was as if a burn had been made in the centre of Diarmaid's forehead.

'There', said the king. 'From now on, any woman who sees that mark upon you will immediately fall in love with you regardless of whom they are, high or low. You can go back to your own land now.'

Diarmaid walked down the tunnel again and came out of the water at the end, at the shore where he had first started. He looked around thinking, 'Things have changed somehow.' But he went on forward and he came upon the camp of the Fianna. In the camp of Fionn he was welcomed very gladly indeed. Everyone was delighted to see him. Diarmaid said to them, 'Why are you so glad to see me I have only been gone three or four days at the most?'

Fionn looked at him and said, 'Diarmaid, you have been gone seven long years.'

From that time on Diarmaid never truly loved any other woman but when a woman discovered the mark on his forehead she loved him. Diamaid became not only the most handsome, the bravest and the kindest of all the Fianna but he also became the one most loved by woman.

# the rescue of fionn's son

It came about in the passage of time that a son of Fionn was captured during one of Fionn's battles against the Lochlannaich to defend the Sons of Morna and the lands of Morvern and Ardnamurchan.

The Lochlannaich, the people from under the sea, were highly skilled workers in stone. Their carvings of plants and animals and of their leaders were wondrous to see. Yet at the same time they were an extremely violent and cruel people.

Their womenfolk were the most beautiful women in the world. They could entice any man of the land to fall for their charms and their nakedness made them even more tantalising. Yet their cruelty was even greater than that of their menfolk, for if they enticed a man of the land to them, when they were done with him (having got what they wanted) they would put him to death by the most extreme torture they could devise. The men of the Lochlannaich on the other hand were excessively ugly. Which may be the reason their women preferred the men of the land – this could be a factor in the hatred they had for the people of the land.

They were also desperate to seize land for

themselves, as their Under Sea World was disintegrating and they knew they must find other areas to live in or die as their world collapsed.

Now they had a great hostage in the son of Fionn and would use him to try to gain from Fionn all they wanted in land and promises.

The Lochlannaich were delighted with their capture and demanded of Fionn that to have his son restored to him he must break his word to the Sons of Morna and no longer defend them, and must allow the Lochlannaich to take over the lands of Ardnamurchan and Morvern.

If Fionn did not comply with their demands his son would be put to a slow agonising death and his body would be cut into pieces and scattered over the Under Sea World. This was a terrible thing to the Fianna for their belief was that if a body was so cut up and scattered it could never be whole again or live in the other world where the spirits went after the change (unless every single piece could be gathered up and re-united, which was an impossible task).

Fionn was caught between two sticks. He wanted to save his son but to do so he had to break his word to the Sons of Morna and the word of Fionn once given could not be broken.

Yet in his mind, the mind of a father, was the great desire to break his word and save his son.

After much thought and heart searching, Fionn decided to send a message to the Old Grey Magician asking him to come and help him solve his dilemma.

The thought had only formed in his mind when from nowhere the Old Grey Magician appeared and said to Fionn.

'I heard your message and felt the pain in your heart. I will do for you all that I can but danger there will be and a cost will need to be paid.'

'To save my son,' said Fionn, 'I will face any danger and pay whatever the cost will be, even to my own life.'

'Then I shall take on the task,' said the Old Grey Magician, 'but you must negotiate with the Lochlannaich to get me as much time as you can. You may have to give them some of their demands to buy time, to save your son.'

Having said this, the Old Grey Magician vanished from the place of Fionn.

The Old Grey Magician returned to his own place to prepare himself for the task that lay before him. He and two of his most trusted apprentices went to the Sacred Grove, a clear space in the middle of a copse of magical trees. Hazel, Rowan, Alder and Honeysuckle with a stone in the centre of the clearing for sacrifice.

There he and they removed their clothing and his apprentices rubbed into every part of his body the oil of anointment he had bought with him. Going to the Stone of Sacrifice he made beside it a small fire from dried leaves and twigs of each type of tree around the grove and the smoke from it rose straight and pure and true into the air bringing to that place even the 'Wisdom of the Bees'.

As his apprentices watched from opposite sides of the clearing he invited the gods to help him in his quest and he laid on the stone of sacrifice his offering of salt, water and food. Asking that it might prove acceptable to the gods.

Knowing now that the gods were with him the Old Grey Magician took on the shape of a great seabird and flew across the moors, the lochs, the hills and the seas to Eilean Mhanainn home of Manannan – god of the Sea (Isle of Man).

On landing on Eilean Mhanainn he reverted to his own shape and made his way to the Court of Manannan and make his plea to him.

He told Manannan how the son of Fionn had been captured by the Lochlannaich and that their

terms to release him were for Fionn to break his
word to the son of Morna and no longer defend
them and give up to the Lochlannaich the lands of
Morvern and Ardnamurchan. If he did not do this
his son would be put to a slow agonising death and
his body would be cut into small pieces and
scattered over the Under Sea World of the
Lochlannaich. The plight of Fionn was that he
wished to save his son but could not break his
word to the sons of Morna.

'I am the god of the Sea,' said Manannan, 'and
I cannot go directly against the Lochlannaich in
this for they are of my realm. Yet I too have a son,
Honi god of the Seaweed, whom I would wish to
save, for on him has been placed an illness which,
while it cannot kill him for he is a god, makes
every moment of his life an agony. I can do
nothing because of a geisa that is upon me. Yet if a
man could be found who would save my son I
would grant him any plea he might make to me.'

'What is needed to save your son?' asked the
Old Grey Magician, 'for I could be that man.'

'Ah,' said Manannan, 'It may be that even you
cannot do what is needed, though I know of your
great magic. You see to save my son you must
bring to me the cup of healing.'

The cup, made by Dianchect (the god of Medicine) in penance for slaying his own son, in which he put the essence of the three hundred and sixty herbs his son became, would cure any illness in the world if drunk from.

'That is indeed a hard task you would put upon me,' said the Old Grey Magician. 'Yet I will undertake it, but in return you must pledge to me that you will give me the use of your Mantle of Invisibility and Forgetfulness to help me save the son of Fionn.'

'If you bring me back the Cup of Healing and cure my son then the use of the mantle will be yours till you save the son of Fionn, and my blessings with it,' said Manannan.

Having the promise he wanted, the Old Grey Magician left the court of Manannan and again turned into the great seabird and flew across the seas, the hills, the lochs and the Moors to the Isle of Skye to the place called Lomharsgil (the place of the magic or shining art), the great centre of Druidical teaching.

Once he arrived there, he made an incantation to gain the blessing of the spirit of the waters of the sea and he stood naked on a rock in the sea which was covered by the water at high tide and called upon the Blue Men of the Minch, his cousins of the sea. The Blue Men of the Minch were the fiercest and most unpredictable of all people of the sea, they lived under the waters of the Minch and if a ship sailed through the Minch they would rear out of the water, grasp the side of the ship and drag it under the waves so that the Minch became known as the Stream of Death and sailors would refuse to sail through it.

The Blue Men of the Minch could talk only in rhyming doggerel and had to be answered and spoken to in the same manner. Standing on the rock the Old Grey Magician stretched his Cromag out to sea and made his invocation:

Three time three rowans now I throw
To wake you from your sleep below
For I your cousin of the land
Must place on you a great demand
And in your hands I place my trust
For travel neath the sea I must

Suddenly the Blue Men of the Minch appeared all round the rock and a fearful sight they were to see:

Blue Men of the Minch are we
We are the warriors of the sea
And though our cousin calls us here
We answer without pledge or fear
We know the place you wish to go
In our dominions far below

The Old Grey Magician said to them:

The cup of healing I must find
To save the god of Seas own kind
And if you help me in this task
From Manannan you a gift can ask

The Blue Men of the Minch answered:

We hear your words and feel your plea
Now you must join us in the sea
And trust in us to show you where
The cup lies guarded in its lair
But you alone must face your foe
If into these dark depths you go

The Old Grey Magician stepped from the rock into
the sea and swam with the Blue Men of the Minch
down, down, down into the deep green depths

where coral reefs and skeletons of ships lay on the sand and great sea creatures swam about and down there were huge black caverns dark and dangerous places. The Blue Men of the Minch led the Old Grey Magician to the mouth of one of the caves and told him:

Within the cave swims a great eel
Who kills those that the cup would steal
No one has left who entered here
So for your safety we must fear
Yet if you come with cup in hand
We'll guard you safely back to land

The Old Grey Magician went boldly into the cave and before long he saw the great eel coiled in front of a pillar of rock on which stood the Cup of Healing. As the huge eel raised its head and glared on the Old Grey magician, he began to weave the crooked end of his Cromag in front of its eyes in a pattern of turns and twists which the eel followed.

Eventually the eel found itself tied into a great knot and as it struggled to untie itself the Old Grey Magician took the cup from the pillar and walked back to the entrance of the cave where the Blue Men of the Minch waited to escort him back to the rock and in the open water of the Minch not even the great eel would dare to attack the Blue men of the Minch.

On reaching the rock, the Old Grey Magician thanked the Blue men of the Minch and said to them:

Your work for Manannan you've done well
So safe you in the Minch will dwell
The peace you seek beneath the waves
He grants and safety in your caves.

But the Blue men of the Minch answered:

To you our cousin of the land
We gladly gave a helping hand
But now we'll rest beneath the waves
For we are free and no one's slaves
Tell Manannan that we wish him well
But we shall choose our way to dwell

Meantime, Fionn had sent Comnhal beul Airgod (Conval of the Silver Mouth) to negotiate on his behalf with the Lochlannaich. Fionn knew that if anyone could charm the Lochlannaich and spread the time of negotiation without giving away too much it was Comnhal, so he put his trust in him. Comnhal was well aware of the difficulty of the task that lay upon him, but he had confidence in his skill and ability to see him through and welcomed the challenge to use his wits against those of the Lochlannaich.

The Old Grey Magician travelled back to Eilean Mhannain to meet again with Manannan and save his son Honi, god of the Seaweed. As he entered the great hall, Manannan himself came forward to greet him.

'You have the cup,' said Manannan, 'Now my son can be cured.'

'Once I have your mantle,' answered the Old Grey Magician, 'I will tell you what you must do to save your son.'

'That was not our bargain,' replied Manannan. 'I said once my son was cured I would give you the use of the mantle and I will stand by that.'

The Old Grey Magician realised he must carry out all the actions required to cure Honi, god of the Seaweed, son of Manannan, to secure the use of the mantle but this would take more time. He could only hope that Conmhal of the Silver Mouth could keep the talks with the Lochlannaich going for the extra time needed.

Now he travelled back to the Isle of Skye to Gleann na Gall and having made his way up the Glen to Tobar Honi (Well of Honi) he made sacrifice, placing salt and food (oatmeal) on the stone above the well and spoke his invocation to it then knelt beside it, and dipping the Cup of Healing into it filled it to the brim from the clean water of the well.

He had to carry the cup back to Eilan Mhannain without spilling a drop and allow Honi to drink from it in the proper ritual fashion. Yet the Old Grey Magician knew that from this time on the gift of healing would be in the water of Tobar Honi because the cup had been dipped in it to be filled

He sealed the top of the cup with a sheet of thin waxed leather tied down with a leather thong so that not a drop could escape and started on his journey back to Eilann Mhannain where Manannan waited.

The Old Grey Magician travelled as fast as he could without spilling any of the water from the Cup of Healing and before too long he stepped again into the Great Hall of the Palace of Manannan and made his way to the throne of Manannan.

Manannan welcomed him with open arms and expressions of his delight and asked that he go immediately to the chamber of his son Honi to let him drink from the Cup of Healing so that he could be released from his pain.

The Old Grey Magician did as he was asked for he had the promise of the Mantle from Manannan and knew his word would be kept.

In the chamber of Honi he uncovered the Cup of Healing, made the incantation to the healing spirit and gave Honi one sup from it. Honi wished to drink it all down but the Old Grey Magician said, 'No, you must empty the cup in three draughts and only when you have done that will the healing be upon you. One you have had, and two more must empty the cup to cure you.'

Honi obeyed the Old Grey Magician and disciplined himself to make three draughts of the cup – not gulp it down. After the third draught the pain left his body and he was restored to his strength and health.

'My work here is done,' said the Old Grey Magician. 'I will take the Mantle and go. The Cup of Healing will not stay with you forever. Until I return the Mantle it will be here, but no one, not even a god, can keep the cup.'

He took the mantle which Manannan gave him gladly and the Old Grey Magician proceeded at great speed to the Under Sea World of the Lochlannaich, to the great city built of white marble in which the face of every building was carved with shapes of plants and sea creatures, and pillars carrying statues of leaders of the Lochlannaich stood beside each door. At the centre of the city was the palace of the leader of the Lochlannaich, the greatest building of all, where the son of Fionn was held prisoner guarded by an escort of well-trained warriors of the Lochlannaich.

Donning the Mantle of Manannan so that he became invisible, the Old Grey Magician walked through the streets of the city and into the palace where he found the dungeon in which the son of Fionn was held. He saw the problem he must solve to rescue Fionn's son.

Two guards were watching over the son of Fionn, one outside the door and one inside the door of the cell. The one outside had the key to the cell, the one inside had a rope from one of his wrists to the tight-bound wrists of the son of Fionn. It would be easy enough for the invisible Old Grey Magician to stun or kill the outside guard and get the key but that would alert the inside guard and he would raise the alarm or perhaps even kill the son of Fionn.

The Old Grey Magician thought for a moment on how to solve the riddle of the guards. Then made his way back down the corridor to a small anteroom where four off duty guards were sitting drinking heather ale from clay pitchers, and as he had noted on the way down they were reaching the sleepy stage. Even as he watched, three of them stretched and yawned and lay down on the sleeping benches and soon were snoring peacefully. The fourth, however, stayed at the table and drank more of the heather ale. The Old Grey Magician decided he must act. He slipped behind the guard and laid two of his fingers on the guard's temple, sending him into oblivion. Then he quickly donned one of the cloaks worn by the guards and lifted two full pitchers of heather ale, but added to each a drop or two from a tiny bottle he carried.

Now he went back to the room of the son of Fionn and his two guards. Stepping up to the one outside the door he said to him, 'We thought you might like these, one for each of you.'

He handed him the two pitchers of heather ale.

The guard was surprised but took them gladly, passing one to the guard inside as the Old Grey Magician had hoped he would. The two guards drank from the pitchers and seconds later lay unconscious on the floor.

The Old Grey Magician quickly took the key and opened the door of the cell and released the son of Fionn who went to rush out of the cell, but the Old Grey Magician commanded him to be quiet and do as he was bid.

They dragged the outer guard into the cell and tied him to the inside guard as the son of Fionn had been tied, then they left the cell and locked the door.

'Let them explain that!' said the Old Grey Magician.

Then the Old Grey Magician discarded the guard's cloak and wrapped the Mantle of Invisibility around both of them, himself and the son of Fionn. They were now invisible and made their way out of the city of the Lochlannaich. The Lochlannaich soon discovered the escape of the son of Fionn and hunted for him, yet if they got too close the Old Grey Magician waved the Mantle of Forgetfulness between them so that they forget what they were looking for and returned to their

city. In this way the Old Grey Magician and the
son of Fionn made it safely back to Morvern.

Back in Morvern, Fionn greeted them with great
delight and hugged his son whom he had thought
he might never see again. Then he recalled
Comhnal na Beul Airgod (Conval of the Silver
Mouth) and asked him what concessions he had
made to the Lochlannaich.

Comhnal said, 'I tried my very best for you
Fionn to help save your son and to gain as much
time as I could.

'First of all I asked the Lochlannaich to define
the exact boundaries of Ardnamurchan and
Morvern. Which took time.

'Then when they laid out their boundaries
I challenged their boundaries and laid out my own.
Which took time.

'Then we argued each boundary difference till
we came to a mutual agreement on the individual
parts of the boundaries in dispute. Which took
time.

'Then we argued out the overall boundaries
in relation to the individual agreements, for as
I pointed out to them, we must determine
boundaries before we can discuss handing over the
land for it both parties do not agree the boundaries

then it leads to future disputes. And that took the most time of all.

'But eventually to gain more time and show goodwill and give proof of integrity, I had to give something to them. So I gave them all the land round the point of Ardnamurchan.'

Fionn gasped.

'Between high and low water!'

'Is that all?' asked Fionn. 'You are indeed Conval of the Silver Mouth, and as you have said so it will be. The Lochlannaich shall have the land round the point of Ardnamurchan between high and low water and their men and womenfolk will not be molested there by any of my people or the sons of Morna. My thanks are with you Conval and you shall not be forgotten.'

After Fionn had made his statement confirming his agreement to what Conmhal had given to the Lochlannaich the Old Grey Magician stepped forward.

'Fionn,' said he, 'you said you would pay whatever the cost might be to save your son. You have not asked what my price is for saving him and for all the dangers I have faced on your behalf. Surely I am worthy of my hire.'

'Indeed you are,' said Fionn, 'and my gratitude

is with you always, and if you need me, my assistance is yours whenever you might call upon it.'

'That is not what I seek,' said the Old Grey Magician. 'What I want from you is your promise that you will give to me the first born child of you and Grainnhe and I will rear it for its first twelve years of life and it shall be famous through all the years to come and shall live to see the end of the world of Fianna and Druid, and of its own change none shall know.'

Fionn was enraged by this and told the Old Grey Magician, 'You ask too much, I cannot give you what you demand and I know not who this Grainnhe is that you speak of. Your request is denied.'

'Fionn,' said the Old Grey Magician, 'you have made of me an enemy who came to you in friendship and gave my assistance to you in your hour of need. I tell you now you will know Grainnhe, but the son you shall have by her will be mine for the first twelve years of his life despite all you might do, and your happiness with Grainnhe shall be brief and bring to you years of grief, yet eventually great pride in your son.'

Fionn ordered his guards to seize the Old Grey Magician but he disappeared as they tried to seize him.

So began the enmity of Fionn and the Old Grey Magician. This enmity lasted for many years and great stories are told of the clashes between them. Yet in spite of this there was between them always a bond which neither could break.

# the death
# of diarmid

*This version of the Death of Diarmid is*
*taken from several tellers in Ardnamurchan*
*about 1942. There is a very similar version*
*which I heard in Skye about 1947. It is set*
*near Sligachan where there are many stories*
*of the Fianna. In both places names of hills*
*and glens are to be found.*

ionn, the great leader of the Fianna, had
met a woman who had rekindled in him
all the fervour of love, and her name was
Grainne. Although Fionn was much older
than Grainne she was happy to be with him
and to marry him.

Fionn was completely and utterly
infatuated with her and called on all his friends
and all of the Fianna to come to his marriage and
share in his happiness and see the amazing beauty
of his beloved.

On the day of the wedding a great crowd
gathered to view the wedding and to give their
blessings on the newlyweds. Even the Old Grey
Magician came despite his problems with Fionn
and gave the bardic blessing on the bride.

After the wedding ceremony all of the company

went to the feast to celebrate the great day and to honour Fionn and Grainne. The main part of the feast was held in the great hall of the King of Morven where all of the Fianna sat round the tables eating and drinking to their hearts' content whilst all the other persons ate at tables set outside round the walls of the Palace of Morven. There was meat of all kinds and finest of wines and spirits of the best with no limit on what any would eat or drink.

The best musicians played both inside the hall and outside that all might dance, and dance indeed they did. Foremost among the dancers was Diarmid, greatest of all the heroes of the Fianna, and he was wearing the leather cap which covered the mark on his forehead which no woman could see without falling in love with him.

It came about that as Diarmid danced with Grainne the leather cap slipped on the sweat of his brow and Grainne saw the mark and fell immediately and totally in love with him.

She returned to where Fionn sat but found an excuse to slip away and talk again to Diarmid. She told Diarmid that she was in love with him and wanted him to take her away from the palace for she would go with him to anywhere in the world, even to the lowest hovel, so long as he was there.

Diarmid refused to do such a thing for it would put shame on his chief and dishonour on himself and Grainne. Yet for all the rest of the night Grainne came back to Diarmid and pleaded with him to elope with her and eventually she told him that if he did not take her away she would shame Fionn before all of the Gathering by announcing that Diarmid had deflowered her before Fionn, and she only married Fionn to have an old man in her bed while she could make love with another.

Diarmid could not see such humiliation placed upon his chief, a man whom he loved, and so he agreed to take Grainne away from the feast and travel with her to places where Fionn might not find them.

When Fionn discovered that Diarmid had fled from the feast with Grainne he was mad with rage and called together all the captains of the Fianna and their followers to go with him to find Grainne and to kill Diarmid. Yet many of the Fianna were on the side of Diarmid rather than Fionn, for they knew that Diarmid had done this against his will and to save Fionn from the humiliation Grainne had said she would put upon him and which she had made a geisa upon Diarmid.

Diarmid had taken Grainne into the lands ruled over by the old king of Ardnamurchan who was a close friend of his, so neither he or any of his followers would reveal to Fionn where or whether they had seen Grainne and Diarmid. There in the place called Glen Hurich Diarmid built two shelters, one for himself and one for Grainne, and round them he built a strong fence with two gates in it, one to the east and one to the west, and he and Grainne settled there for a time. But their time there was short for the hunters and trackers of the Fianna found the place and brought Fionn and the Fianna to it.

Fionn stood outside the fence and called upon Diarmid to say whether he and Grainne were inside the fence and Diarmid, who could speak no lie, said they were and he would come out by the gate he chose.

After he had said this the Old Grey Magician appeared inside the fence and offered to take Diarmid and Grainne out of the enclosure under cover of his cloak of invisibility, but Diarmid refused, yet asked that Grainne be taken out in this way, so the Old Grey Magician took Grainne safely out. Then Diarmid went to the gate to the west and asked who stood there.

'Whoever we are,' he was told, 'we will let you out safely and go with you to Fionn to plead your cause.'

'That is not the way for me,' said Diarmid. Then he went to the east gate and asked who guarded it.

'This gate is guarded by Namhan and his sons who hate the very ground you walk on, and by Fionn himself and his sons and grandsons,' came the reply.

'Then this is the gate I leave by,' said Diarmid, and he launched himself into the air in the leap of the heroes, soaring over the heads of the Fianna and landing beyond them. Before they gathered their wits he was out of their sight among the trees and the hunt for him had to start again.

Diarmid met up again with Grainne in the place where the Old Grey Magician had left her for him. The best hearted of men could not forsake her, so together they travelled farther into Ardnamurchan to the great forest below Beinn Resipal and above Loch Shiel. Deep in the forest stood Luis (the tree of magic, the rowan). It was guarded by a surly giant who allowed no one near the tree, but Diarmid, by his charm of manner and honesty, persuaded the giant to allow himself and Grainne to climb the tree and live among its branches. Diarmid wove together a shelter for each of them from the branches in such a way that that they could not be seen from the ground. The Giant had told them that the one thing they must never do was eat of the rowan berries for if they did it would bring grief and death and a greed that could never be quenched, for always they would want more yet know not what they wanted.

It came about that one day Fionn and some of the Fianna were hunting in the forest and they sat down around the Tree of Magic to rest and eat some food. After they ate Fionn and his son Ossian had a game of chess to pass the time before the hunt resumed. Their chessboard was set on the ground below the tree and the game reached a stage where Fionn was winning, but one move could change that and make Ossian the winner, so Fionn challenged Ossian to find that one move. Diarmid, who had been watching the game from above, knew the move that should be made and seeing Ossian was baffled dropped a rowan berry so deftly that it hit the piece that should be moved. Ossian took the hint and moved the piece and won the game. This happened twice more, but Fionn had spotted what was going on and he looked up

into the tree and asked if Diarmid was there.
Diarmid answered that he indeed was there and
Fionn immediately set his men in a ring around the
tree to stop Diarmid's escape.

Even as the ring was being set up the Old Grey
Magician arrived in the tree in the shape of a crow
and once again took Grainne to a place of safety.
Then Diarmid called out to Fionn and walked to
the very end of a branch and so light was his step
it barely bent. Once again he carried out the Leap
of the Heroes and cleared the perimeter of the ring
of the Fianna and escaped.

Now, however, the Old Grey Magician took a
hand. He went to talk to Fionn, pointing out to
him that wherever Diarmid had stayed with
Grainne he had made two shelters so that they did
not sleep together, so clearly he had behaved
honourably and not betrayed Fionn. He also
pointed out to Fionn that most of his captains of
the Fianna were in favour of Diarmid and wanted
a reconciliation between them. If Fionn agreed to
such a treaty he would get Grainne back and gain
admiration for his statesmanship and strengthen
the Fianna by bringing back to it its greatest
warrior. He also warned Fionn he must be sincere
in bringing back Diarmid, for if he was not and

tried to kill or injure Diarmid under the guise of friendship it would bring about the end of the Fianna.

Fionn was persuaded by the arguments of the Old Grey Magician and a meeting was set up between him and Diarmid and Grainne. At the meeting Grainne told Fionn that she was being returned to him as she was when she left him. Fionn and Diarmid embraced again as brothers and together walked back to where the Fianna waited.

Grainne however, being a woman, had longed for what she could not have and had taken an opportunity to eat some of the berries from the tree of magic and now felt herself to be a woman scorned by Diarmid, so she started to work on Fionn, telling him that Diarmid was going to take the leadership of the Fianna from him and that he should make a plan to get rid of him before he did this. She kept on at Fionn like a dripping well.

Eventually Fionn made a plan and asked Diarmid to join him and some others of the Fianna in a hunt in Kintyre, and Diarmid, to help their new friendship, agreed. They went down to Kintyre and had good fun and good hunting but then one evening as they relaxed after that day's

hunt Fionn said to Diarmid, 'One beast I have
hunted but never managed to kill is the Wild Boar
of Beinn Ghuillan and here we are just over the hill
from it. Could it be that you, great hunter as you
are, could do what I could not?'

'As you know,' replied Diarmid, 'I have a geisa
upon me that I may not kill any boar so I cannot
do this for you.'

'Is it that you are afraid to do it?' said Fionn,
'Perhaps some of the others would rather die trying
than be deemed coward.'

'Coward I never was,' said Diarmid. 'Tomorrow
I will slay the Boar and bring you its skin.'

The next morning Diarmid went to Beinn
Ghuillan and after some trouble slew the Great
Boar and skinned it. He took the skin of the boar
to where Fionn was and spread it before him and it
was a huge skin.

'Will you pace it for me?' asked Fionn, and
Diarmid paced the skin of the Boar. 'Can you pace
it again?' said Fionn. 'And this time do it from the
tail to the head for I cannot believe the size.'

Diarmid paced the skin but this time one of the
poisoned spikes on the spine of the skin pierced his
heel, the only place where he could be wounded,
and he fell dying.

Now Fionn remembered the good times they had had together and sorrow came upon him, and he went to where Diarmid lay and asked if he could help him. Diarmid told him if he brought his cupped hands full of water from the well at the shore and let him drink from them he could be saved. Fionn rushed down to the well by the shore and filled his cupped hands but when he reached Diarmid he remembered what Grainne had said and he opened his hands letting the water run onto the ground. Then as he looked again upon Diarmid he remembered the words of the Old Grey Magician and again he ran to the well at the shore and filled his hands he came to the side of Diarmid's head ready to let him drink, but as he looked on the face of Diarmid he recalled the hurt of searching for Grainne and he opened his hands letting the water soak into the ground beside Diarmids face. But then again sorrow came upon him and he rushed again to the well and back to Diarmid and tried to make him drink, but it was too late for Diarmid was dead.

So began the end of the Fianna, for many of his captains would no longer follow Fionn after such treachery.

# fionn
# and
# grainnhe

rainnhe was the daughter of the King of Morven and the granddaughter of Caileach Ruagh na Sithean (the Old Red Woman of the Fairies) and of all the maidens who ever walked the slopes of Alba or the green turf of Erin she was the most beautiful and the purest.

The old Grey Magician however hated all that was good and wove his enchantments about her so that she could not leave her father's house without the protection of the spells of her grandmother. There came however the day when she left the house without such protection and was instantly carried off to the land of the Grey Cold Darkness.

Now Fionn was in his favourite place, Glenelg, and was playing at putting the stone with some of the other Fiennes when there suddenly appeared before him an old woman in a tattered red cloak – the colour of royalty.

'Great Fionn', she said. 'I have come to put a task upon you who are the defender of the innocent if you will but take it'.

'Tell me your task,' said Fionn, 'and if I think it to be just I will take it upon me'.

Then Caileach Ruagh na Sithean told Fionn of the abduction – of Grainnhe by the Old Grey

Magician and asked that Fionn the perfect one in
whom was no evil would rescue Grainnhe and
bring joy back to her sorrowing grandmother and
father. Then Fionn, knowing that he would have
to travel alone to the land of the Grey Cold
Darkness from which he might never return, took
upon himself the tasks of rescuing Grainnhe and
bringing back joy to her grandmother.

When he took his vow the old woman gave to
him three things to help him on his return: a needle
off a fir tree and two pebbles – one white and
polished so that it sparkled; one black and jagged
and dull. Great is the magic of these, she said, and
you will know how to use them when your need is
great.

Having told this to Fionn a gust of wind from
the west picked up the old woman and carried her
off and as she went she grew smaller – like a
swallow skimming, then like a bee, then the tiny
dot of a spider on a silken thread, then like the
black spot in your eye which vanishes when you
blink she disappeared from the sight of men.

Then Fionn set off for the land of Grey Cold
Darkness with only his sword Mac-an-Luinn (Son
of Light) for company. For days he travelled till his
provisions were near finished and he had but two

grains of oatmeal left. He sat below a tree to eat them and as he did a hoarse voice croaked: 'A bit for me Fionn for my need is great.' Looking up he saw the great raven of the wilderness perched above him and he gave to it one of the grains, saying, 'Your need is as mine, friend of the wilderness.'

Then croaked the raven: 'I am forever your friend; when you need me I will be there,' and it flew away.

Fionn, refreshed by his grain of oatmeal, continued on his way but soon the hunger came upon him again and what did he see on the shore but the great grey seal of the west. Drawing his sword he leapt forward to kill it but before he could do so the seal spoke and pleaded for its life, saying, 'Hold your hand great Fionn of the good heart for I have mouths to feed and if you kill me you kill the defenceless ones who have done you no harm.'

Then Fionn, hungry as he was, sheathed his sword and told the seal to go in peace. The seal swam away only to return in a twinkling of an eye with a great salmon in its mouth.

'This is for thee, Fionn, friend of the helpless, and when you need me I shall be there.'

So Fionn spitted the salmon upon his sword and

roasted it and ate well. But after eating he felt like a bone was caught behind his tooth and when he put his finger behind the tooth to flick out the piece of bone he found that he could see that which was, and that which is, and that which will be, and he realised that he had eaten of the salmon of knowledge and the knowledge was his now whenever he needed it, and he continued on his way.

He came now to an area of barren rocks where no grass grew nor any trees or shrubs and knew he was coming near to the land of the Grey Cold Darkness. As he walked on his foot struck a rock, knocking it over. From beneath the rock dashed a little mouse who squeaked at Fionn, 'Why have you destroyed my home, Great Fionn? I do you no harm.' Just at that a great eagle swooped from the sky and scooped up the mouse in its talons. But even as it rose again into the air the hand of Fionn closed upon it.

'Release the mouse,' said Fionn, 'for I will not have the death of it upon me.'

The eagle released the mouse and soared away in anger but Fionn called to it, saying; 'Do not be angry with me you of the all-seeing eye for I am pledged always to defend the weak and helpless,' but the eagle did not answer him.

Then the mouse said to him, 'Great Fionn, take me with you to the land of Cold Grey Darkness and I will help you.'

'How you can help me I know not,' said Fionn, 'but if you wish to come with me you shall,' and he picked up the mouse and sat it on his shoulder in the folds of his plaid.

Now he came to the edge of the barren land, where the sea stretched to the misty land of Grey Darkness, but the sea between boiled and seethed with strong currents so that no man not even great Fionn could swim it and there was not as much as a leaf to make a boat from. As Fionn stood there looking and wondering how he might cross there appeared upon the shore the Great Grey Seal of the West.

'I told you when you needed me I would be there. Jump upon my back and hold tight and I will take you over to the land of Grey Darkness.'

So Fionn got upon his back and the seal carried him across the water to where he wished to be. 'When you return I will be here,' said the seal and it dived back into the water.

Fionn moved on in this strange, grey land and felt the cold of it seeping into his bones but his task he would fulfil so he kept bravely on. Now he came to a great maze of rocks which were so great he could neither see over them nor throw them aside but he knew he had to get through them to find the castle of the magician. As he started into the maze he heard a raucous noise above him calling, 'Look up, Fionn, and follow me.'

There above him flew the Great Raven of the Wilderness. So Fionn watched and followed it as it flew and so he came through the maze of stones in which many had died.

On the far side of the maze in the distance could be seen the castle of the Old Grey Magician but to approach it closely was impossible without being seen and Fionn knew if he was seen the Magician would put a spell on him and Grainnhe that would stop him rescuing her. Then spoke up his friend the little mouse.

'No man can enter the castle, Fionn, but I can and I will listen and come and tell you all I hear,' he said, and he scuttled away into a crack in the rocks.

Soon he was back and told Fionn that luck was with them for that very night was a great feast in the castle and all in the castle would be asleep by the early hours of the morning. He had seen Grainnhe and she was tied by a rope to a pillar in the great hall of the castle but he would gnaw through the rope when all were asleep and lead Grainnhe out to where Fionn waited in the rocks.

The plan went well and Grainnhe joined Fionn at the edge of the maze. Together they fled to the shore where the Great Grey Seal of the West took them upon its back and swam across the rough boiling sea to put them safely ashore-upon the barren land. When they looked back they saw that the Old Grey Magician was aware of their escape and was in pursuit of them in the shape of a great grey whirlwind. They began to run but Grainnhe could not run so fast as Fionn so he put her across his shoulders and kept on running. Fionn, however, was not the fastest runner amongst the Fiennes and when he looked back the Grey Magician was catching up on him.

Fionn remembered the things Cailleach Ruagh na Sithean had given to him and from his sporran he took the needle of a fir tree and without breaking his stride he placed it in a crack in the rocks. When he looked back again a great wood had appeared between him and the Grey Magician so high it could not be jumped and so wide you could not get around it so the Grey Magician had to find his way between the trees. So Fionn kept on running and gained some ground.

Next day when Fionn looked back he saw that the Grey Magician had changed to the shape of a host of armed men and was again gaining on him fast. Fionn took from his sporran the polished white stone and without breaking his stride placed it upon the ground and kept on running. When he looked back the stone had turned into a great loch the surface of which was so polished that it reflected the sun so that the armed men were blinded by the light of it and had to wait for darkness before they could continue their pursuit of Fionn. So Fionn again gained ground.

Next day when Fionn looked back the Grey Magician was once again overhauling him just as Fionn took from his sporran the jagged rough black stone and without breaking his stride placed it upon the ground. When he looked back again a range of high peaked mountains had appeared between him and the Grey Magician too high to jump over and too wide to go around so they must be climbed and Fionn kept on running for he knew that ahead of him was the great red river (Allt Dhearg Mhor) and if he could cross it he and Grainnhe would be in safety till they reached Glenelg.

When they reached the bank of the river they looked back and saw that the Grey Magician had overcome the mountains and was advancing upon them but the river was so wide and strong that not even great Fionn could swim over it so he drew Mac-an-Luinn, his sword of light, though he knew its power would be useless against the Grey Magician and all his own magic was used up.

Grainnhe had in her hair a great red jewel and this had two gifts in its power. It could keep the wearer safe so long as they wore it or it could grant the wearer one wish. Grainnhe took the jewel from her hair and looked into it and saw what her future would be if she made the wish she wished to wish, but she was already in love with Fionn so she chanted her incantation to the stone:

*Tha'n d'uisge farsaing*
*Cha-n-eil mi thairte*
*Cha-n-eil mi feuim an sgiath iolair*
*Thoir thoisir mo fheinn eathar urrain dhomh dha*
*'S iomar tarsainn 's mise 's mo gradh*

The water is wide
I cannot get across
Nor do I have the wings of an eagle

Bring to me a small boat fit to carry two
And we will row across my love and I

After she had sung her wish Grainnhe placed the
jewel on the surface of the river where it turned
into a small boat and by the time the Grey
Magician reached the bank Grainnhe and Fionn
were more than halfway across and safe from his
spells.

Together then they travelled back to Glenelg
where they were married and lived happily
together for some time till just before Grainnhe
gave birth to their first child. Just before the child
was due, Fionn received a call for help from the
Sons of Morna whom he had promised to assist
against invaders whenever they needed him. Now
they called on him to help repel the small dark men
who were invading them and he must go or break
his word.

Though Fionn was gone for only three days
when he returned he found that Grainnhe had been
taken by the Grey Magician and by placing his
finger to his Tooth of Wisdom he discovered she
had been changed into a pure white hind. Far and
wide Fionn and the Fiennes searched for Grainnhe
but no sign did they find for the Grey Magician

had hidden her in the most remote vastnesses of far Glen Affafaric.

Twelve years passed and one day as Fionn and his men were hunting they came upon a small copse of trees. Bran the great dog of Fionn suddenly turned upon the hounds, nor would he let any hound or hunter save only Fionn himself into the copse. When Fionn entered the copse he found in the centre of it a boy of twelve years who could make only the sounds of the deer and in the centre of whose head was a patch of deer's hair in a wave down his forehead where his mother had licked it. Fionn looked into the face of the boy and saw the face of his beloved Grainnhe and knew this was his son. He took the boy home to Glenelg where he learned the ways of men and became one of the greatest warriors of the Fionn and the greatest bard who ever lived and his name was Ossian.

In time there came the news that Grainnhe had died and the Grey Magician said that if Ossian came to his land he could bring back the body of his mother. Ossian went to the land of the Grey Cold Darkness and brought back the body of Grainnhe, restored now in death to all her beauty, and the Fiennes dug for her on top of a hill in Skye looking to her beloved Glenelg a grave and in the grave they placed each one the jewel most dear to them in a great urn.

There Grainnhe lay and in a great cave below her in their time came the Three who knew not Death (An Triannan) – Fionn and Ossian and one other to sleep till they were needed to bring back to Scotland all its power and former glory.

# lochlannaich

fter the Old Grey Magician returned from saving the son of Fionn he thought over the things he had seen and done.

He thought on the great city of the Lochlannaich below the sea and how he had seen signs of the deterioration of its protection, and he knew that before too long the protection would give way and the city would be engulfed and the Lochlannaich would be wiped out.

Yet in his heart he felt that the loss of such highly skilled and creative craftsmen would be a disaster for all mankind, and that he should try to preserve their race and skills. Perhaps he also felt their preservation would be an annoyance to Fionn.

After considerable thought he arranged a meeting with leaders of the Lochlannaich, despite the danger to himself.

At the meeting he told the leaders that he knew of the desperate search they were making to try to seize land for themselves before their world collapsed, but as they must know, their strength in arms was not enough for them to capture and keep the land for themselves, especially with Fionn and the Fianna defending the sons of Morna.

The only result of their raids was to weaken their numbers and all they had to show for them was the land between high water and low water round the point of Ardnamurchan which they had been tricked into. They must change their tactics and find a new plan if they were going to maintain the succession of their race. The leaders of the Lochlannaich had to admit the Old Grey Magician was correct that their numbers were too low to take and hold land, but they had no other plan to ensure that their race continued and they also knew that the time their world would survive was short and that they would die without it.

Unless the Old Grey Magician had a plan?

'I have a plan,' the Old Grey Magician told the Lochlannaich, 'but it is one that will take time to carry out and will mean a change in your way of life. My plan is this! The skills you have in stonework and metalwork are inherent in you and are passed on to your children and grandchildren. Already you have amongst you some who are born of unions between your people and people of land. If they are matched again to a third generation and that third generation are reared as people of the land with people of the land, they will be accepted and will get land upon which to carry on your blood and your skills.'

'That may be true,' said the leader of the Lochlannaich, 'but how do we get the third generation to be accepted and reared as people of the land?'

'That is a large part of my plan,' said the Old Grey Magician. 'I will persuade the people of the land, perhaps those who cannot bear children or have lost children, to take and rear as their own some of your third generation children and they will give your people a foothold amongst the people of the land. In time your descendants will have land to live in. It may not save your present generation but it will ensure your skills and blood are carried on in times to come.'

The leaders of the Lochlannaich took some time to discuss the plan and decide how to answer, then spoke again to the Old Grey Magician.

'We are willing to accept and try your plan', they said, 'but we would make some conditions of our own if it is to go ahead. Firstly, we have six young females here who are of second generation between us and people of the land and are of an age to bear children. You must lie with them so that your seed is in them and ties you to them, for no good man will easily forsake his own children and it will also preserve your own succession.'

'Secondly, you must give us your promise that you will ensure that as many as possible of the third generation of children are fostered by people of the land.'

'To save your race,' said the Old Grey Magician, 'I will accept both your conditions. The first will be a pleasure and honour to me and the second I already intended to carry out if you accepted my plan. You must also promise that where unions are made between people of the land and yourselves that the people of the land will be returned safely to the land.'

'Then we are agreed,' said the leaders of the Lochlannaich, and so it was that the Old Grey Magician, lay with the six maidens then returned to his home and made arrangements for his children and other children of similar unions to be fostered by people of the land.

Before many years had passed and by the time the undersea world of the Lochlannaich had collapsed a good sized colony of the mixed breed of the Lochlannaich and the people of the land existed and were known for their skill in stone and metalwork.

Yet they were also known for their seafaring skills, and were not a settled people for even on the land they travelled to different places living from their skills and creativity in working in metal, stone and timber.

They were given many names and in Argyll were known as Sheonies which was sometimes translated as people of the seaweed or shore.

# spirits of
former days

quiet lies the Glen beneath the summer sun
No roar of mindless city life
No sound of gun
But neath the pleasant smiling face
Lies history of wild primeval wrath
The pride of race
And overhead against the blue arched sky
The lazy soft fringed clouds
Blow swiftly by

Come winter and the wild wind's eerie howl
Brings fingers cold upon your spine
And thoughts that prowl
To tales of long ago when yet the world was new
Of giants of the little folk
Who legends grew
And in your mind there grows a fearful doubt
Were all the magic and the mystic spells
Truly worked out

The long cold winter nights draw slowly on
There's time to feel the forces of the earth
Before the dawn
And in your head the swirling thoughts revolve
Softening the fabric and the strength
Of your resolve

So from the darkness comes the answer true
What's gone before lives on though changed
To spirit hue

And as you live so close to nature's normal law
The very rocks emit an air
Of power raw
And in the force-field of the earth's magnetic rays
You learn to touch again the spells
Of former days
No longer strange there beams upon your mind
The wandering restless spirits
Of a former kind

Accepting then the sense of power unseen
One blends in with the present
What has been
And in the gloom of winter on quiet moor and glen
Thoughts set free to wander where they will
Meet thoughts of former men
So forming pictures of the days so long gone by
Like flick'ring images upon a TV screen
Plucked from an empty sky

Lost to the city dweller now the sense that captures
    from the air
The swell and surge of battle dark
Or legend fair
That from a hundred or ten thousand years before
Come back again in sounds of winters strife
Or sea waves roar
Yet now and then even men of science reveal
They can dimly sense the knowledge
The mystics knew as real

Although the sense grows strong in winter's
    darkest days
Throughout the spring there lingers in the air
The scent of passed by ways
And even in the midst of bright summer's balmy
    heat
There comes the fading echoes
Of the past's heart beat
And in the soft wrapped swirl of warm mist and
    rain
We stop and listen to the murmurs
Of a lost refrain

# afterword

# ossian reclaimed

DONALD SMITH

# fionn and the fianna

he stories of Fionn and his warrior band are a mainspring of traditional culture in Scotland and Ireland. The Fianna are a very mixed bag – noble and brutish, handsome and ugly, grizzled and fresh faced. Diarmaid the impossibly handsome and honourable beguiler rubs shoulders with the knottily muscled and thuggish Goll Mac Morna. Fionn's son Ossian is a poet and dreamer, nursed by an enchanted deer, while Ossian's son Oscar is the epitome of this-worldly martial valour. There is Bald Conan whose bulging waistline belies his native cunning, and slender Caoilte the runner who can outstrip the speed of thought. These characters clearly have their origins in a world of gods and giants, but come to inhabit narratives in which heroism, magic and human folly intertwine.

Women in this realm are always larger than life; supernaturally beautiful or hideously aged; devoted or enchanting and downright dangerous. Yet threads of psychological motivation run through the cycle mingling with powerful passions in a way that stays in the memory. Decisive episodes are embodied in poetic lays or ballads as well as prose tales. Storytellers and reciters probably mixed music, poetry and prose when performing the big tales. These tales have survived in many different versions in oral memory and in print. The traditions of oral performance go back to the Fianna themselves who, in addition to their fighting skills and athletic prowess, were lovers of poetry, song, storytelling and music, accompanied by lashings of food and drink.

The point of the stories is to entertain through a kaleidoscopic play of action, mood music, verbal wit and natural colour. There are some constant values in the tales such as desire for the free life of hunting, fairplay, the need to take on challenges however strange, love of beauty and courage and a refusal to fear death. However there is no didactic intention. The later stories, often recited by Fionn's son Ossian to St Patrick, are nostalgic for a lost world of heroism and freedom. They remind us that the traditions of Fionn were passed on and recorded by clerics after the onset of Christianity which influenced this later more explicitly spiritual tone.

The stories of the Fianna cannot be tied to any specific location or time. Storytellers position the tales, including places of birth, death and burial, according to the purpose of the telling and to suit the audience. The cairns of memory are multiple; Diarmaid's tombs are legion. Equally the stories are not historical even when they may reference historical circumstances in the passing.

Because many of the stories reference 'the Lochlannich' as inveterate foes of the Fianna, some historians have placed the tales in a period when it is suggested bands of roving warriors were required to fight off the Vikings. But as the material in this book shows, the Lochlannich are supernatural dwellers beneath the waves as much as flesh and blood warriors. Often in Celtic lore it just depends what side of a multifaceted jewel you display to the light at any given moment. The point is that there must be enemies – Northmen, fellow Celts or underworld beings all serve their turn – and if that fails the Fianna can always fall out amongst themselves.

Moreover the Viking theory would put Fionn and his band in the ninth century onwards, but the stories are layered with beliefs and behaviour from earlier centuries, while written and oral versions evolved through further centuries. Though Ossian and St Patrick appear as the principal medieval narrators in respectable literary sources, Fionn has a much longer prehistory and now a revivified post-Christian existence as well.

That said, when John Francis Campbell and his associates collected Fionn ballads and tales in Scotland in the 19th century, the tradition bearers they recorded were insistent that Fionn had been a real historical figure, and that they were relating a traditionary history, not fiction or fantasy. Of course many of the same individuals believed in the Bible as the ultimate historical authority. Within informal community networks, the Fionn stories possessed a cultural validity comparable to the authority which sacred scripture commanded in church and school. In that sense the storytellers' claim for the truth status of their art is fully justified.

From the time of the Protestant Reformation in Scotland in 1560, the church attacked and suppressed the traditional culture of the people, thereby acknowledging it as a rival. John Carswell, Bishop of Argyll and the Isles in the time of Mary Queen of Scots, specifically denounced vain tales of the Fianna which were clearly very popular among his errant flock. We can understand that, since the stories are still alive in modern collections and in

the performances of live storytellers on the margins
of a technologically dominated culture.

## scotlanò anò irelanò

Unfortunately in modern times Fionn and his band
have been the victims of misunderstanding and
prejudice. I have referred already to the emergence
of Puritanism after the Scottish Reformation and
its assault on traditional culture. But this played
into a much wider prejudice against the Celtic way
of life in Scotland and Ireland. In this scenario
savage 'natives' are pitted against the forces of
modern civilisation which became aggressively
imperialist in their acquisition of land and
resources. Religion, language and education
became weapons in the drive to break the will and
spirit of native culture. After the failure of the
Jacobite Risings in 1715 and 1745–46 the attack
in Scotland became systematic and brutal, resulting
in many Highlanders emigrating through choice or
compulsion, as glens were cleared of people in
favour of the landlord's sheep and deer.

A predominantly Protestant and increasingly
industrialised Scotland backed the Protestant
Union with England and the British Empire. Even

the martial tradition of the Highland clans was subsumed into the imperial cause. In this process Fionn and his band were depicted as Irish, not Scottish. In fact, everything that was distinctive about Scotland's Gaelic culture was ascribed to Irish influence, a perspective epitomised by the belief that the original 'Scots' were fifth century invaders from Ireland. As 19th century Ireland diverged from Britain politically and culturally, Irishness in Scotland became tainted by prejudice, and associated with nationalism or 'papistry'. Finn and his warrior band were well on the way to becoming 'Fenians'.

The problem with these assertions is that in the cold light of day there is no archaeological or historical evidence for any invasion of Scotland from Ireland. On the contrary, the evidence is that Argyll and other parts of south-western Scotland had a culture similar to Ireland from prehistoric times, and that what we now describe as 'Celtic' developed in both countries in parallel, regardless of the legendary claims of self-promoting royal dynasties. That is also exactly what the geography suggests, especially as, for centuries, the sea provided the main roads. This exchange of people and culture has been continuous from the earliest movements of human population to the present.

Moreover there is ample evidence that a long established Gaelic speaking culture in Argyll and south western Scotland had strong ties through trade, dynastic alliance, war, culture and religion with both the British Celtic peoples of southern Scotland and the Pictish Celts of northern and central Scotland. Though they fought with each other, it was on the same cultural terms. Gradually, through the influence of Christianity and the pressures of Viking attack, those groups of native kingdoms coalesced into what is recognisably the modern nation of Scotland. Far from being subordinate to or derivative from Ireland, Scottish Gaelic culture was a leading force in the formation of Scotland and its distinctive institutions, culture and identity. Influences moved between Scotland and Ireland in both directions.

The Fionn stories in Scotland reflect this context. Firstly they are close cousins of the Arthur tales. In his earlier incarnations – the British Celtic ones – Arthur is god, giant and rude hero all in one, accompanied by his warrior team. Only much later under Norman-French influence does Arthur become a medieval king surrounded by knights.

Early Arthur traditions abound in southern Scotland but are also present in Pictish areas and in Argyll, where Clan Campbell claims descent from Diarmaid of the Fianna and Arthur! The clear sense is of shared cultural influences without strict demarcations of geography or language.

Consequently, to the present day, the Arthur and Fionn stories are embedded in landscape features and place names across Scotland. These often occur in clusters rather than in isolated instances pointing to a close relationship between early mythology and beliefs about the creation and shaping of the land. Though it is impossible to accurately date all these associations, many are longstanding and cannot be ascribed to one period in which an incoming Irish culture re-spun the Scottish landscape.

In fact, early Irish myths and sagas incorporate Scotland or Alba as a related but different place. Cuchullin, the archetypal Irish bruiser, goes to Skye to pit himself, in every sense, against the warrior queen, Sgiath; Columba goes to Alba in exile, and Deirdre and the Sons of Uisneach seek refuge from the reach of Conchobar King of Ireland in Argyll, which is clearly not an Irish colony.

It is obtuse to conflate the all-important Gaelic
aspects of Scotland with 'Irish influence'. This was
a distortion cultivated by detractors of Scotland's
Celtic character, though strangely some in
Scotland's Gaelic speaking communities perpetuate
the same mistake with careless talk of 'the Gaels'
– Scottish and Irish – as if they were some unified
race apart from the rest of Scotland. That is to
undermine, not reaffirm, the historic and
continuing place of Gaelic culture in the Scottish
mainstream; a culture formed over many centuries
of interaction between different geographic and
cultural influences, including Norse settlement in
many parts of the Highlands and Islands. The
Gaelic language itself is a critical indicator of
Scottish distinctiveness, not a regional sideshow.

## OSSIAN MACPHERSON

By the mid-18th century Fionn and the Fianna had
been pushed into the cultural background, but in
the 1760s an ambitious young man from Badenoch
set the heather ablaze with his *The Poems of
Ossian*. James MacPherson turned the Fionn of
Highland tradition into Fingal, hero of the
incipient Romantic Movement's first international

blockbuster. The impact was enormous, catapulting a newly hatched Scottish Celticism into the forefront of European culture. In the United States Thomas Jefferson lauded Ossian, and Napoleon was to sleep with the book under his pillow. All that had appeared backward, barbarous and blameworthy in the Gaelic world was, it seemed, turned to advantage, and even the mixed performance of the Jacobite Prince Charles Edward Stuart in 1745–46 was subsumed into the new European cult of 'the noble savage'.

This was not a haphazard development. MacPherson was brought up in the aftermath of Culloden, experiencing repression and depression first hand. While studying at the University of Aberdeen he was taught by the brilliant Rev Thomas Blackwell, who pioneered analytic criticism of the Homeric epics, identifying how Europe's first and foremost poet had fashioned his masterworks from earlier traditional sources.

When James MacPherson published his first modest efforts at translation of traditional Gaelic sources, *Fragments of Ancient Poetry* (1760), the Scottish Enlightenment literati rushed to his side on the scent of 'a lost Scottish epic'. Their motivation was patriotic, seeking to replace

Scotland's lost political independence, and its recent history of civil war and revolt, with intellectual and artistic achievements that would outshine the defeats. MacPherson cleverly obliged. What neither party anticipated was the worldwide hunger for primitive, noble values that would lead many to latch onto James MacPherson's bold reinvention of the Fionn sources, hailing them as the authentic expression of a former, purer age.

MacPherson was fully aware of the Fionn stories and ballads which were still a commonplace of his local Gaelic culture, even as it came under huge external pressures. Equally his refashioning of those sources into 'the lost epic' was wholly conscious. He needed to introduce the kind of consistent characters and tragic coherence which was exemplified by Homer, but absent from the much looser cycles of Fianna tales. However, the scale and nature of the response must have taken the young aspirant author by surprise. MacPherson was restoring Gaelic pride and presenting Scottish culture in a way that he knew would be acceptable to refined and enlightened tastes. But people seized on the primitive authenticity of Ossian as the essential seedbed of Romantic inspiration.

At the same time patriotic Scottish support for *The Poems of Ossian* provoked an English counter-attack, fronted by the foremost literary authority of the day, Dr Johnson. In consequence, James MacPherson was left defending not the quality of his literary work but the validity of his sources. All parties in this controversy ought to have known better, but that could be said of most of the *causes célèbres* which generate extensive heat but little light. Johnson, courtesy of James Boswell, was to experience the Scottish Highlands and their civilisation at first hand. In literary critical terms he had a valid point about MacPherson's work, but that became mired in anti-Scottish prejudice such as the claim at one juncture that Gaelic had no written literature.

MacPherson in turn had boxed himself into a corner by claiming too much. Having begun by emphasising oral tradition, he resorted to claiming a manuscript source, eventually translating his imaginative English reinventions back into Gaelic, instead of pointing to his actual Gaelic inspiration – the widespread Scottish tales of Fionn and the Fianna. The dispute became bogged down in issues about manuscripts, and which ones MacPherson had seen or not seen. Many of the classical manuscripts however would have needed specialist knowledge to decipher.

One positive side-effect of the controversy was that people in the Highlands began to collect and preserve the ballads and tales. When the pioneering folklorist, John Francis Campbell, studied the Ossian traditions in the 1860s he was able to cite more than twenty existing manuscript collections, as well as hundreds of direct transcriptions of orally recited Fionn stories and songs recently gathered from many parts of the Scottish Highlands. The accusation that MacPherson had made the whole thing up was from the very beginning ridiculous, and progressively unsustainable as more and more people came forward with examples of his sources.

But the main, enduring consequence of the Ossian controversy was to relegate the Fionn stories to an ambiguous shade. Not only did it sideline genuine traditions which had been culturally central in the Scottish Highlands, but it undermined any other possibility of using the original materials in wider contexts. The local Gaelic storytellers continued as before unaffected by MacPherson's book which they did not read, while devotees of the Romantic Ossian were not interested in any other less Heroic versions. The loser in this fracas was Scottish Gaelic culture, and its role in the Scottish mainstream.

MacPherson himself died a wealthy man, able to buck the general trend by buying an estate in his native Badenoch. However, though the immense cultural influence of the *Poems of Ossian* is widely acknowledged and studied, MacPherson's actual writings are now unread and according to some unreadable. By contrast Fionn and his band remain in rude health, ripe for very different rediscoveries and reworking. Scotland can and should reclaim Ossian for its own.

## OSSIAN RECOVERED

This book contains a group of stories and traditions relating to the Grey Magician or 'An Buidhseir Glas'. The Magician, referred to in Irish sources as the Dark Druid, is a key figure in the Fionn cycle. He is an inveterate enemy of Fionn and responsible for abducting the mother of Ossian. Yet the Grey Magician is a shadowy rather than defined figure of threat, endowed with magic but apparently unmotivated powers. In previous Fionn collections there is no explanation of the origins of this figure or the reasons for his enmity. But in the central tale of this collection 'The Rescue of Fionn's Son', both of these things are addressed and explained in the traditional manner – by providing another story.

'The Rescue of Fionn's Son' is an important and fascinating episode in the Fionn cycle, and mainstay in the repertoire of a contemporary Scottish Highland storyteller, George Macpherson. In this volume he gives a detailed account of the sources of the tale and of how over his own lifetime he heard the different elements at different times and reconfigured the full story.

George Macpherson is a tradition bearer of the same clan as James MacPherson, though his family is descended from Macphersons who provided the bodyguard and later standard-bearers for the Chief of Clan MacLeod in Skye. There they settled in Glendale which was later to play a major part in the 19th century struggle for Highland land reform. Glendale has a rich tradition of storytelling in which George's family has played a notable part. George himself was born in Greenock but spent much of his childhood with relatives in Ardnamurchan where he heard the first part of 'The Rescue of Fionn's Son'. He also has family connections in Argyll where he spent much of his working life, retiring to Glendale where he has devoted nearly three decades to the traditional culture and the wellbeing of the local community, not least the pioneering, crofter owned Glendale estate.

In 1989 George Macpherson was one of the first traditional storytellers to be invited to The Netherbow Arts Centre in Edinburgh to share stories in the context of an international festival of oral storytelling, and since then his presentations of Highland culture through storytelling have been in demand nationally and internationally, contributing to a renaissance of this ancient oral art. Unlike many contemporary storytellers, George Macpherson eschews dramatic embellishment in favour of the focussed delivery of traditional sources. As George's public role as a storyteller was recognised, people of the older generations in Skye have increasingly shared long remembered stories with him in the hope of keeping them alive.

There are several valuable contributions that George Macpherson makes to our understanding of the Fionn traditions as a whole. Firstly, he is an inheritor of the unbroken tradition of storytelling which John Francis Campbell delineated so fully in the 19th century. Secondly, he belongs to a distinctively Scottish tradition that draws on several areas of the Scottish Highlands and Islands. The main external influence on the Grey Magician tales is from the Isle of Man, which as we shall see is highly significant. Thirdly, the content of his stories is rich and illuminating in its own right and in terms of wider appreciation of the cultural background. George Macpherson is reclaiming Ossian from his literary predecessor James MacPherson, and giving renewed life to Fionn and the Fianna in continuity with the oral tradition bearers.

## the old grey magician

The stories in this collection add an interesting dimension to the Scottish Fionn cycle in terms of motivation and sequence. But they also extend our understanding of the rich mythological background. In George's account of reclaiming 'The Rescue of Fionn's Son', curiosity about the creatures of the sea whets his desire to hear the story. In his tale the Old Grey Magician has to go to the Island of Manannan, god of the sea, in order to find a way of loosening the grip of the people of the sea, the Lochlannich, on the people of the land.

Who is the Old Grey Magician? The Gaelic 'Buidseir' refers to a bird, the Great Grey Shrike, and 'Buitseach' to a wizard. This shrike is a solitary bird of prey, a migratory bird, with distinctive grey and black markings. It is not a common bird and must always have attracted notice. The Old Grey Magician in George Macpherson's tales shape-shifts into a great grey bird to travel over sea and land. Significantly, to rescue Fionn's son he has to go to the Isle of Man (Manannan), familiar in older tradition as the Island of the Druids.

In Irish Finn stories, the equivalent of the Old Grey Magician is the Man of Darkness, of secret powers and druidry. The Irish name also spans two related meanings, dorcha or doirche/darkness and doirte/druid. Like the Dark Druid, the Grey Magician is not a god, but a human in tune with spiritual powers and energies. Such a figure is a 'magus' in the sense that his extraordinary abilities are founded on esoteric knowledge that can only be gained through special disciplines and insights.

George Macpherson himself sees the Old Grey Magician as a survival of druidic beliefs and traditions. This relates both to the Magician's paranormal abilities and to the nature of the Fionn tales through which characters and events in their physical manifestations are fluid and ever-changing. The unity comes from a constant spiritual energy expressed through the flow of the story, and of one story into the other. This expresses a continuing belief that there are two planes of existence – the world of physical phenomena subject to change, and a plane of spiritual energy in which nature also participates. Spirit life can move between the two planes, and those with druidic disciplines and insights are go-betweens. In this regard, Celtic druids belong in the wider context of shamanic beliefs and practices in Europe and Asia.

The storyteller in turn acknowledges this spiritual philosophy through the practice of his or her art. The 'spirit life' is reincarnated in each telling, and the shared communion of teller and listeners in the tale reunites the material and spirit worlds through a shared energy. This includes all aspects of life from rough humour to profound love, humanity and the wider life of nature. It is an art of metamorphosis and transformation which draws us into a deeper sense of our existence within a universe much wider and stranger than dreamt of in our everyday presumptions. Those who have listened to George Macpherson's storytelling can sense this underlying philosophy and intent without necessarily being able to describe the beliefs it embodies. He has sustained both the distinctive content of the Fionn tradition and also its spiritual purpose and function.

All of these underlying aspects of the tales are vividly focussed in motifs of healing. The Old Grey Magician has to cure the son of Manannan god of the sea if Fionn's son is to be rescued. For this he needs both the cup of healing and the water from the well of Honi, god of seaweed and the fertility of the sea, so binding sea and land in mutual health. The cup of healing is prominent in these tales and was later to be taken up into the medieval Arthurian lore of the Holy Grail. It is profoundly significant that, in 'The Death of Diarmaid', Fionn's betrayal of healing causes the death of Diarmaid by letting the life-giving water slip between his fingers, so fatally undermining the fellowship of the Fianna.

Those familiar with more recent written popularisations of the Fionn stories will find differences of detail as well as overall intent and purpose in George Macpherson's traditional sources. For example, Ossian's mother, who is enchanted and abducted by the Magician/Druid, is Grainnhe, already established in this story as Fionn's wife. Alexander Carmichael, working at this time in collaboration with John Francis Campbell, heard a similar account from Donald MacPhie, a blacksmith on Barra and an accomplished storyteller, in 1866. Campbell wondered aloud about the relationship between this Scottish story and Grainnhe's part in the death of Diarmaid. That however would be to expect a logical linear progression which is foreign to the Fionn cycle as sustained by the traditional tellers.

It is instructive and satisfying to encounter both these tales from George Macpherson's present repertoire in this collection. Each story recreates the world afresh in a continuum of change. It is James MacPherson's *Ossian* that pursues consistency and a fixed literary status that is foreign to oral storytelling's intimate connection with the fluidity and fertility of life in all its forms.

## **Luath** Press Limited

*committed to publishing well written books worth reading*

LUATH PRESS takes its name from Robert Burns, whose little collie Luath (*Gael.,* swift or nimble) tripped up Jean Armour at a wedding and gave him the chance to speak to the woman who was to be his wife and the abiding love of his life. Burns called one of 'The Twa Dogs' Luath after Cuchullin's hunting dog in Ossian's *Fingal*. Luath Press was established in 1981 in the heart of Burns country, and now resides a few steps up the road from Burns' first lodgings on Edinburgh's Royal Mile. Luath offers you distinctive writing with a hint of unexpected pleasures.

Most bookshops in the UK, the US, Canada, Australia, New Zealand and parts of Europe either carry our books in stock or can order them for you. To order direct from us, please send a £sterling cheque, postal order, international money order or your credit card details (number, address of cardholder and expiry date) to us at the address below. Please add post and packing as follows: UK – £1.00 per delivery address; overseas surface mail – £2.50 per delivery address; overseas airmail – £3.50 for the first book to each delivery address, plus £1.00 for each additional book by airmail to the same address. If your order is a gift, we will happily enclose your card or message at no extra charge.

**Luath** Press Limited
543/2 Castlehill
The Royal Mile
Edinburgh EH1 2ND
Scotland

Telephone: 0131 225 4326 (24 hours)
email: sales@luath.co.uk
Website: www.luath.co.uk